DATE DUE

Michel Schooyans

THE

DEMOGRAPHIC

CRASH

From Fatalism to Hope

Translated by

Rev. John H. Miller, C.S.C., S.T.D.

ISBN 1-887567-16-X

Published by
The Central Bureau, CCVA

Printed by St. Martin de Porres Lay Dominican Community
New Hope, KY 40052

ABBREVIATIONS

BPCL:	*Bioethics and Population: Choose Life*
CA:	*Centesimus Annus*
DC:	*Documentation Catholique*
DLC:	*Democratie et liberation chretienne*
ECOSOC:	Economic and Social Council
ECA:	Economic Commission for Africa
ECE:	Economic Commission for Europe
ECLAC:	Economic Commission for Latin America and the Caribbean
EPA:	*L'Enjeu politique de l'avortement*
ESCAP:	Economic and Social Commission for Asia and the Pacific
ESCWA:	Economic and Social Commission for Western Asia
EV:	*Evangelium Vitae*
FAO:	Food and Agriculture Organization
GS:	*Gaudium et Spes*
ILS:	Interactive Information Service
ICPD+5:	International Cairo Population and Development + 5
ILO:	International Labor Organization
IPPF:	International Planned Parenthood Federation
INSTRAW:	International Research and Training Institute for the Advancement of Women
HABITAT:	UN Center for Human Settlements
TTL:	*The Totalitarian Trend of Liberalism*
UNAIDS:	Joint UN Programs for HIV/AIDS
UNDP:	UN Development Programs
UNEP:	UN Environment Program
UNESCO:	UN Educational, Scientific and Cultural Organization
UNFPA:	UN Fund for Population Activities
UNHCR:	UN High Commissioner for Refugees
UNICEF:	UN International Children's Emergency Fund
UNIFEM:	UN Development Fund for Women
RN:	*Rerum Novarum*
SC:	*On Social Concerns*
UN:	United Nations
WHO:	World Health Organization

i

TABLE OF CONTENTS

APPENDICES

INTRODUCTION

The purpose of this book is to explain as clearly as possible the drop of fertility rates worldwide. Why are women having fewer children? Why is the growth rate of the population diminishing? Why is the population ageing? These phenomena are seen practically everywhere in the world. Sometimes, as in Europe, they show the traits of a *crash*. This word is especially rich in meaning. It habitually evokes the plummeting of an airplane. As we will demonstrate in the first three chapters, fertility and the birth rate are, in effect, rapidly declining to such an extent that we can indeed speak of a crash.

Furthermore, as we learn from the famous Webster dictionary, the word *crash* can also evoke a sudden bankruptcy of an enterprise or the collapse of a society. In a decidedly suggestive way, Webster's dictionary further indicates that the word *crash* also designates a period of elevated mortality and of a marked decline in living persons. As a result of the ageing population, this problem is increasingly prevalent among human beings. Finally, when the English word *crash* is used as an adjective, it has the connotation of urgency: a situation thus qualified is so grave that we must do something as quickly as possible with maximum utilization of all resources available. We couldn't say it better.

Applied to population, the word *crash* evokes the rapid fall in fertility and birth rates. The very clear drop of these indicators is a recent enough phenomenon, and can be explained by increasingly numerous interventions to control the transmission of life. Our demographic decline is taking the form of a disaster, a shipwreck: if man is dying out, what is the future of the world? Why this decline? Why this collapse? What consequences will it entail?

Our study, however, will have to go beyond the mere analysis of the decline of demographic growth. Therefore, we have devoted two chapters (IV and V) to an analysis of the activity of the UN, the principal promoter of population control policies. In this self-assigned task, the UN relies on the assistance of its agencies or organs as well as the support of powerful nongovernmental organizations. With remarkable consistency the international organization convokes innumerable meetings whose common aim is to curb the growth of world population by any means.

We are not going to limit ourselves to describing the principal conferences of the last few years. We will analyze the ideology behind demographic control, which underlies all the programs of the international organizations. The hard nucleus of this ideology has certainly shown a remarkable stability. Nevertheless, over time and during the international conferences, diverse themes have been incorporated, for better or for worse, into the first versions of this ideology. In their quest for legitimization, the actual programs organized with an authoritarian demographic agenda have certainly not been unfaithful to Malthus, but they now use terminology such as "new rights of man," "reproductive health," "gender," "new family models," "Mother Earth"—without forgetting the omnipresent and magical term *consensus*.

Confronted by such powerful organizations, one is strongly tempted to simply throw in the towel. Others may dream of the UN and its satellites becoming "Babelized": it cannot be denied that the confusion of languages will (really and figuratively) take over, that the Third World will rebel, or more prosaically, that Moloch will fail. As for ourselves, we believe that it is urgent to undertake systematic action to prevent every totalitarian measure which bears the law-and-order ideology of demographic control. Accordingly, the last three chapters will suggest actions individuals or organized groups can undertake to confront this immense peril. Let's not mince words: we are providing a detailed plan for *lobbying* on behalf of life.

Louvain-la-Neuve, August 1999.

CHAPTER I

THE DROP IN FERTILITY THROUGHOUT THE WORLD

In the middle of the film *Titanic,* there appears a particularly impressive scene. The oceanliner has just hit the iceberg; the hull has been ripped open. Once informed, the captain sends for the engineer who built the ship to examine the damage. With the plans of the ship in hand, the engineer quickly gives his diagnosis: more water is coming in than the pumps can dispose of. "What's going to happen, then?" asks the unfortunate captain. "The *Titanic* is going to sink. That is a mathematical certainty," the engineer emphasizes. This is precisely what happened, despite the blindness of those who, contrary to the facts, obstinately declared the ship "unsinkable."

The *Titanic's* catastrophe was avoidable. It was only necessary to abstain from deliberately making a decision which was dictated by pride: namely, the determination to opt for the straight route, shorter but more dangerous due to the icebergs, rather than take the oblique route, longer and therefore proffering less *panache*. They should have seriously considered the radio message indicating the presence of icebergs, as well as investigate why lookouts and lovers alike shivered from the cold, etc. Above all, they should have abandoned the idea that the ship was unsinkable, a Promethean and fatal conviction since it courted the insane gamble of defying death.[1]

Without giving in to panic, we wonder if the odyssey of the Titanic is not a grave signal for the entirety of human society. For if there are foreseeable catastrophes, like that of the *Titanic*, there are others, which are not only foreseeable, but announced, as well, such as the one we are going to treat. The point common to both cases is that the catastrophes are avoidable, on condition that the relevant reports are objective and taken into account, that adequate measures are taken, and finally that people have enough courage to ward off what ignorance, sloth, and perhaps bad faith present as an inevitable.

SOME KNOWN AND INCONTESTABLE PHENOMENA

Drop in the fertility index

The drop in fertility rates as well as the decline in population growth are two phenomena which have been observed for many years by demographers whose scientific authority is well-established. Without entering into detailed explanations, let us recall that the expression *synthetic index of fertility* (SIF) is used to define the median number of children born to women of childbearing age. In those countries having the highest health care standards, each woman of childbearing age must have an average of 2.1 children in order for the population to be replenished. This index is declining practically everywhere in the world. One sees this in industrialized countries as well as in developing countries.

Fall of natural growth rates

The same tendency holds true for the rates of natural population growth. This formula expresses in percentages the rise or fall of the population. A population that, from one year to the next, increases from a size of 100 to a size of 101 indicates a growth rate of 1%. Like the synthetic index of fertility, the natural rate of growth is in decline the world over.[2] Illustration 1 shows the evolution of this rate with projections based on a median hypothesis of the United Nations.

These two phenomena were observed and analyzed ages ago, notably by Alfred Sauvy. For the case of France, they were studied in detail through the examination of French demography in his work, *La France ridée*[3] (France Shriveled Up). Gerard-François Dumont announced *L'Hiver démographique*[4] (The Demographic Winter), while in his book, *Festin de Kronos*[5] (The Banquet of Kronos), he has investigated the generalized European population decline. The same author analyzed the world demographic fall and its consequences in *Le Monde et les hommes*[6] (The World and Men). Similar observations were made by Daniel Noin in his *Atlas de la population mondiale*[7] (Atlas of World Population), as well as by Yves-Marie Laulan in *Les Nations suicidaires*[8] (The Suicidal Nations). These findings have also been reported in several widely circulated publications.[9]

Illustration 2 offers a resumé and visualization of the decline in fertility rates in the major regions of the world from 1950-55 to 1998. On

Illustration 1

Evolution of growth rate of world population

1950-2050

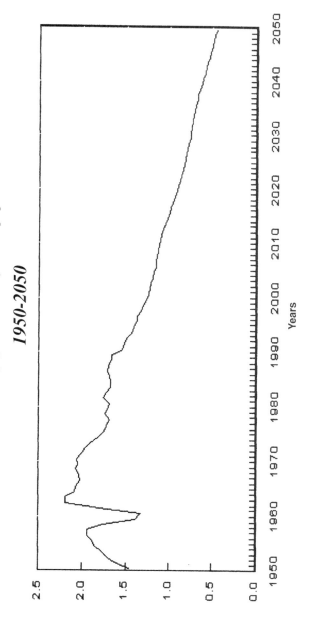

Years

Source: U.S. Census Bureau, 1999, International Data Base.

a scale of 0-8, the table tracks the number of children among women of childbearing age between 1950-1998.

Neomalthusianism disputed

A number of well-respected authorities acknowledge these facts. For instance, Rafael M. Salas pointed out the tendency to fertility decline in *Reflections on Population*.[10] The World Bank also admits the same facts, without, however, admitting all the consequences.[11]

Monographs devoted to the fertility decline are not yet very numerous. However, the one written by George Martine about Brazil presents certain methodological interest, even if this attentive demographer for obscure motives minimized, if not erased, the influence and extent of the programs for controlling the population in this country.[12] In the United States, Julian Simon, recently deceased,[13] and Gary Becker, who received the Nobel Prize in economics (1992),[14] have demonstrated in their learned studies the increasing scarcity of "human capital," the principal wealth of industrialized countries and the motor of all development.

Illustration 2

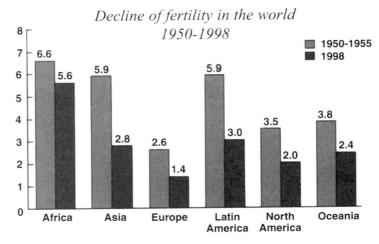

Decline of fertility in the world 1950-1998

Source: Alene Gelbard, Carl Haub and Mary M. Kent, "World Population Beyond Six Billion," *Population Bulletin* 54, 1 (March 1999) published by the Population Reference Bureau, Washington, D.C.; see p. 14.

The list of specialists who have sounded the alarm is unexpectedly long. Nonetheless, their conclusions have been habitually hidden by the media and ignored by some decision-makers. Because of them, the entire world has been subjected to an unprecedented deception in the history of ideological manipulation: the world is on the brink of a "demographic explosion" and this threat creates a "state of necessity" for voluntary and even quasi-authoritarian control of the world population.

The myths of "demographic explosion" and of "exponential growth of world population" continue to be spread with loud constancy by certain technocrats of the UN, especially of the UNFPA, the World Bank, the WHO, and the UNPD, who reap the dividends of this hoax. But this is not the place to begin the critical analysis of what we call "the ideology of demographic security."[15] Our intent is more limited. We start with a simple observation: in the neomalthusian choir of the UN and its agencies, some discordant voices have recently been heard. We focus our attention above all, but not exclusively, on an event of outstanding importance. The prestigious Division on Population of the Economic and Social Council of the UN, in effect, invited to New York, from November 4 to 6, 1997, a group of top international demographers in order for them to compare their views on the drop in fertility rates in the world.[16] We were glad to observe once more the remarkable independence of spirit of the Division on Population.[17] This organ is characterized in effect by its scientific requirements to which other UN agencies sometimes prefer falsified ideology.[18]

What is striking in all the contributions of this working session is the convergence, even unanimity, of the report. Certainly, interpretations vary, but one fact was admitted as indisputable: fertility is falling all over. The contribution of Jean-Claude Chesnais is especially remarkable, and his conclusions were widely corroborated by the other demographers present.

Hence, the moment seems opportune for us to examine this fertility drop, its causes, its consequences, and the remedies we can bring to bear on it.

We will take advantage of three types of works: first and foremost, those of demographers who have discerned the problem for a long time; then communications at the New York meeting, especially that of Jean-Claude Chesnais; and finally some information recently made available on the internet. Such is the case of the graphics of the Census Bureau of Washington, whose data from May 1999 we are using.[19] In sum, we will by and large let the facts speak for themselves.

THE AGE PYRAMIDS

Structure by age

In order to sensitize people to the fertility drop and the "demographic implosion," the most expedient way to proceed is to show the different *age pyramids*. Without going into detail, let us recall that these pyramids provide a representation of the structure by *age and sex*[20] of a given population. This structure can be expressed in relative numbers, as in Illustration 3. The pyramid represents, in this case, for example by percentages, the *proportion* of men and women in relation to the total size of the population. This structure can also be expressed in absolute numbers, as in Illustrations 4-10. The pyramid represents the *number* of men and women according to age in the total size of the population. The addition of all the age brackets and classes is equal to 100% of the total size of the population.

What we wish to set in relief, thanks to the pyramids that follow, is the tendency of the population to get older rather than the evolution of their sizes.

In our illustrations, each line or rectangle represents the population by brackets of five years. Thus we successively have, on the left, beginning at the bottom, a line representing one group, as it happens the ensemble of boys who have their age from 0 to 4 years in common; above this line are represented boys of 5 to 9 years, and so on to the oldest. On the right appear the corresponding groups of females. The entirety of the bars, or the total surface of the rectangles, represents 100% of the population under consideration.

It should be remarked that these pyramids are full of objective lessons. They allow us to visualize at a glance the presence of a more or less large group in such and such an age bracket. It also allows us to compare one group with another, younger or older, or again a group of men with one of women in a given year. The results of war appear in some pyramids in which the male population of such an age bracket is clearly lower than the corresponding female one. The same effect can be observed in countries in which many men emigrate to find work in foreign lands. An example of the latter case appears in Illustration 11 in which we see that, in the age bracket of 25 to 34 years, the size of the Hispanic population in the USA is visibly larger than the corresponding

8

size of the female population. Inversely, female infanticide, sometimes practiced, is perceptible in the comparison among certain male and female groups of the same age brackets.[21]

The fact must also be emphasized that, apart from the compensatory support from immigrants, the size of each group represented by a line cannot but diminish, for the population accounted for in each group is necessarily subject to a certain rate of mortality. Also the population of 0 to 4 years, represented by the base of the pyramid, will be irreversibly represented by a shorter rectangle once this group has passed to the 5 to 9 age bracket.

The pyramids also provide us with another objective lesson: They demonstrate the importance in a country of the *dependent population*. While simplifying, we should realize that this expression refers habitually to the population of below 20 and over 64. This population depends for life and survival on the support of the active population.

In a general fashion, the structure by age, that is, the distribution of the population according to age brackets, varies according to whether we are considering industrialized countries or those still developing. Illustration 3 clearly shows that the proportion of youth is larger in developing countries than in industrialized ones.

We display these two pyramids because of their didactic interest: they illustrate what we have been explaining. In reality, they are so general that their demographic interest is very limited. Each country and region has a population that has its own profile.

We are going to present the pyramids of a few countries, developed as well as developing. For these different examples, we have recourse to the pyramids published in August of 1998 by the Census Bureau in Washington, D.C. The Bureau's demographers first of all constructed the age pyramid for 1996, and then, assuming that the tendencies then particular to each country would remain constant, the Census Bureau calculated what the population of these countries would be in 2025 and 2050. The results of these calculations appear in Illustrations 4 through 10.

France, Italy and Spain

We will first display the pyramids for three developed countries: France (Illustration 4), Italy (Illustration 5) and Spain[22] (Illustration 6).

Illustration 3

*Decline of fertility in the world
1950-1998*

Developing Countries

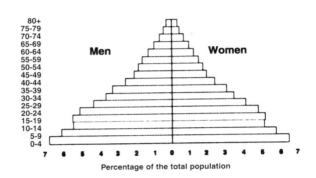

Percentage of the total population

Developing Countries

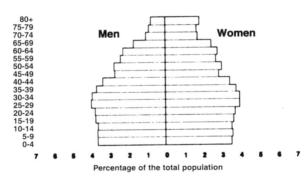

Percentage of the total population

Source: United National Population Division, 1992, data from 1990, according to the World Resources Institute, Washington, DC, 1999; address: http:/www.wri.org/wri/enved/trends/pop-1d.html

10

Illustration 4

Age Pyramids for France

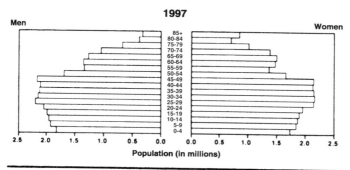

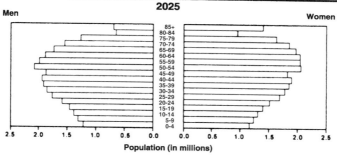

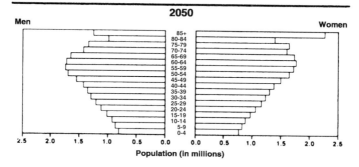

Source: Census Bureau, Washington, D.C., 1999

Illustration 5

Age Pyramids for Italy

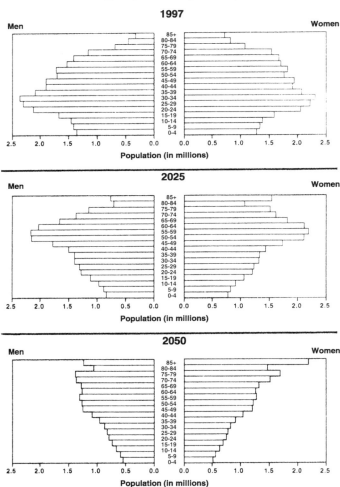

Source: Census Bureau, Washington, D.C., 1999

Illustration 6

Age Pyramids for Spain

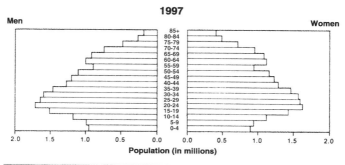

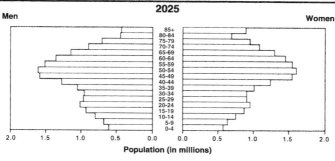

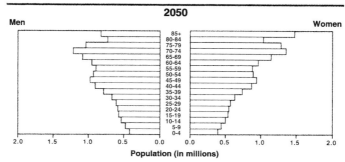

Source: Census Bureau, Washington, D.C., 1999

China, Mexico and Brazil

One would believe that the tendency in the decline of fertility rates is to be seen only in wealthy countries. That is not true. See what the age pyramids for China (Illustration 7), Mexico (Illustration 8) and Brazil[23] (Illustration 9) have to say.

Illustration 7

Age Pyramids for China

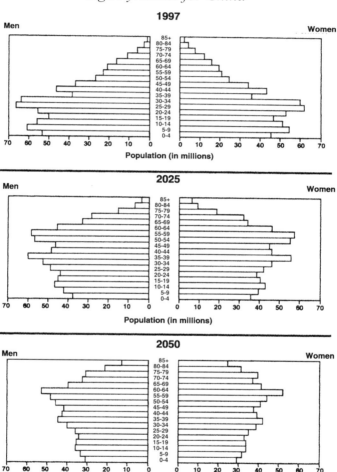

Source: Census Bureau, Washington, D.C., 1999

Illustration 8

Age Pyramids for Mexico

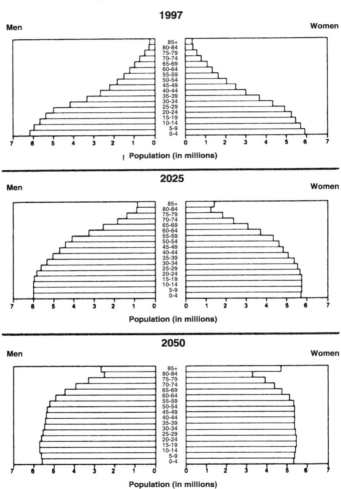

Source: Census Bureau, Washington, D.C., 1999

Illustration 9

Age Pyramids for Brazil

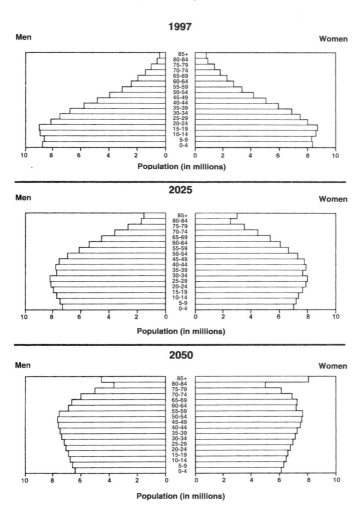

Source: Census Bureau, Washington, D.C., 1999

The Case of the USA

The case of the USA deserves to be cited due to its distinctive feature. In effect, for 2050, the age pyramid shows only a slight tendency toward shrinkage at the base. See Illustration 10.

Nevertheless, when we analyze the situation more closely and consider the data of 1996, two things are apparent. First, the pyramid of the North American non-Hispanic population shrinks at the base. But the pyramid for the North American population of Hispanic origin has an age structure clearly younger with a very wide base (see Illustration 11). That indicates that from 1996 to 2050, the proportion of the Hispanic population will have doubled, as Illustration 12 shows.

Illustration 10

Age Pyramids for U.S.A.

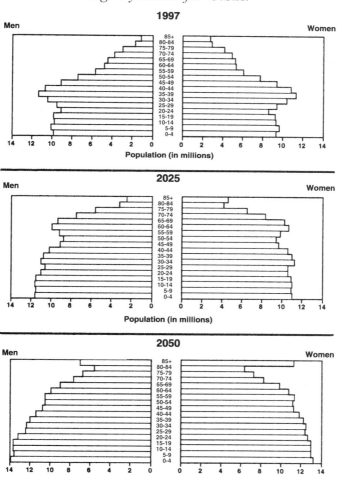

Source: Census Bureau, Washington, D.C., 1999

Illustration 11

Age Pyramids for Hispanics and Non-Hispanics

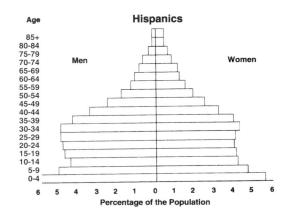

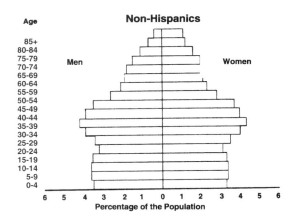

Source: Jorge del Pinal and Andrey Singer, "Generations of Diversity: Latinos in the United States," *Population Bulletin* (Washington, D.C.) vol. 52, n. 3 (Oct. 1997) 16.

Illustration 12

*USA: Proportion of the Hispanics and Other
Populations in 1996 and 2050*

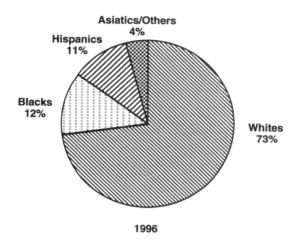

1996

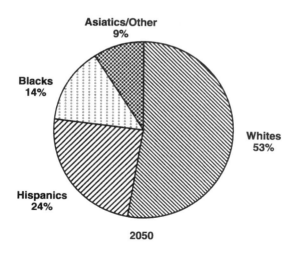

2050

Source: ibid. (Ill.11) p. 14.

[1] There is another disastrous example. The *Vasa*, the ship commanded by the king of Sweden, Gustavus II Adolphus (1594-1632), was intended to impress all the kingdoms of the Baltic by its presence and its 64 canons. Moreover, it was supposed to be "the artistic expression of the power" of Sweden. Victim of an error in conception aggravated by a ballast of insufficient weight, the vessel, due to a strong wind, sank in 1628 in the very port of Stockholm upon its inaugural voyage. It was an avoidable catastrophe also resulting from human error, and a consequence of megalomaniac bravado.

[2] For more explanation of these various notions, see our work, *Pour comprendre les évolutions démographiques*, 2nd ed. (Paris: University of Paris-Sorbonne, Association for Research and Demographic Information, 1995).

[3] Paris: Pluriel, 8335E, 1979.

[4] The expression, launched by G. F. Dumont, was taken up as the title of a book devoted to Europe and published under the direction of François Geinoz (Lausanne: ed. L'Age d'homme, 1989).

[5] Paris: Fleurus, 1991.

[6] Paris: Litec, 1995.

[7] Montpellier: Reclus, 1991; see esp. pp.20 f.

[8] Paris: Xavier de Guibert, 1998.

[9] From among the publications that have taken up this problem, let us cite the article "Voici la verité: la natalité ne se redresse pas. Le cri d'alarme des démographes," in the *Figaro Magazine* n. 799 (Feb. 17, 1996) 28-35; one should also keep in mind the dossier prepared by Gérard-François Dumont (pp. 30-35) and the article of Denis Lensel (p.35). See also Jacques Dupaquier, "L'Europe malade de sa démographie," *Population et Avenir* (Paris), May-June 1999, p. 2f. For its part *Le Monde* in *Économie*, April 7, 1998, published a dossier organized by Yves Mamou entitled "Le vieillissement, source de déclin?" pp.I-III. See also the article by Jacques Bichot and Michael Godet, "Le tabou démographique," in *Le Monde*, April 14, 1998; and that by Richard Dubreuil, "Dénatalité: le piège se referme," in *L'Homme nouveau* (Paris), n. 1189-1190 (Aug. 2-26, 1998) 1 and 3. See the dossier by Renauld de Roche-Brune about Africa, "Population. En route vers les 10 milliards," published by *Jeune Afrique* (Paris), Oct. 27-Nov. 2, 1998, pp. 46-53. Attentive to the demographic evolution, the Pontifical Council for the Family elaborated an important point in "Déclaration sur la chute de la fécondité dans le monde"; it was published in *L'Osservatore Romano* n. 11 (March 17,1998) 9 f. Taking *The State of World Population 1998* (New York: UNFPA, 1998), *Le Monde* in its issue of Sept. 3, 1998, carried the headline: "L'Explosion démographique de la planète n'aura pas lieu." And the UNFPA was forced to acknowledge the decline in fertility rates, but hurried right away to offer sacrifice to its old demons. The ageing of the population is also recognized by the WHO, see especially the article "Ageing: the Surest Demographic Reality of the Next Century" in *World Health* (Geneva) n. 2, 1998, 26 f. A comprehensive dossier on "La population mondiale en mutation" was published in *Le Monde, Dossiers et Documents* n. 227, June 1999.

[10] New York: Pergamon Press, 1986, esp. 11-16 and *passim*. The same observation was made by George B. Simmons and Ghazi M. Farooq in the introduction of the collection work of which they were the editors, *Fertility in Developing Countries* (London:

Macmillan, 1998) 7-9. This work refers especially to Amy Ong Tsui and Donald J. Bogue, "Declining World Fertility: Trends, Causes Implications," in *Population Bulletin* 33 (Oct. 1979) n. 4.

[11] See *Health, Nutrition and Population* (Washington, D.C.: The World Bank Group, The Human Development Networks, 1997) 91.

[12] See George Martine, "Brazil's Fertility Decline," *Population and Development Review* 22 (March 1, 1996) 47-75.

[13] See especially *L'Homme, notre dernière chance* (Paris: PUF, 1985) 177-179; also *Population and Development in Poor Countries* (Princeton University Press, 1991) 138.

[14] Above all see *A Treatise on the Family* (Cambridge, MA.: Harvard University Press, 1993).

[15] See our Chapter V. Also cf. our works: *The Totalitarian Trend of Liberalism* (At. Louis, Mo.: Central Bureau, 1991) 37-59; *The Gospel Confronting World Disorder* (ibid., 1999) 153-173.

[16] The documents concerning this meeting bear the title *Expert Group Meeting on Below-Replacement Fertility* (New York: United Nations Secretariat, Population Division, Department of Economic and Social Affairs, Nov. 4-6, 1997). Several documents discussed come from the Population Division itself; the other documents are due especially to Jean-Claude Fesnais, Michael Teitelbaum, Paul Demeny, Jurgen Dorbritz and Charlotte Hoehn, James McCarthy, Joe Murray-Lawless, Antonio Golini, Ryuichi Kaneko, Sergei Zakarov and Jiang Zhenghua.

[17] The Population Division of the Department of Economic and Social Affairs regularly publishes scientific reports on world population. See *World Population Prospects: The 1996 Revision. Draft* (New York: Secretariat of the United Nations) Three volumes: 1. The Text properly so-called, January 1998; 2. Appendix 1: Demographic Indicators, Oct. 24, 1996; 3. Appendix II and III: Demographic Indicators by major area, region and country, Oct. 24, 1997.

[18] Among others on this subject see Ben J. Wattenburg, "The Population Explosion is Over," *New York Times Magazine* Nov. 23, 1997; Nicholas Eberstadt, "World Population Implosion?" *The Human Life Review* 24, 1 (Winter 1998) 15-30.

[19] Address: http://www.census.gov/ipc/www/idbnew.html

[20] See our work *Pour comprendre les évolutions démographiques* 2nd ed. (Paris: University of Paris-Sorbonne, 1995) 33-35. For more details see Gérard-François Dumont, *Démographie* (Paris: Dunod, 1992)

[21] We take up this question later in Chapter II under *Sterilization*.

[22] On the demographic decline in Spain see Manuel Ferrer Regales and Juan José Calvo Miranda, *Declive demografica, Cambio urbano y Crisis rural. La transformaciones recientes de la población de España* (Pamplona: Universidad de Navarra, 1994).

[23] Regarding Asia one can refer to the works of Rose Linda G. Valenzona, "Demographic Trends in Selected Countries in the Asia and Pacific Regions," *International Conference on Demography and the Family in Asia and Oceania*, Acts of the Congress of Taipei, Sept. 18-20, 1995 (Taipei, 1996) 89-119. She has also produced a thoroughly researched study on *The Empty Cradles of Asia*, a duplicated manuscript (Manila, 1995?). See also Betsy Hartmann, *Control* (Boston: South End Press, 1995), especially Chapter IX: "China: 'Gold Babies' and Disappearing Girls."

CHAPTER II

WHY THIS DECLINE?

The decline in fertility rates is hardly an incomprehensible phenomenon eluding human understanding. We are going to set forth some of its causes. We will group them under two major headings: the not very propitious climate for fertility, and the impact of anti-birth techniques.

AN UNFAVORABLE ENVIRONMENT

1. We observe first of all that people marry later in life. It follows that the median age at which women have their infants rises. This tendency to delay marriage has, without any doubt, several causes. Among them figures the lengthening of life expectancy, which has experienced a spectacular boom in the twentieth century. In Mexico, for example, life expectancy at birth was 27 years at the beginning of the century; today it is close to 75 years.

2. There are fewer marriages than before; this is the so-called *drop in marriages*. Before getting involved in a pregnancy, women want to have a minimum assurance of the father's fidelity and a minimum of assurance with regard to public services. To raise a child is, in effect, an enterprise that is spread out over a long period.

3. On an entirely different level, *women's access to all levels of education*, especially higher education, is also a cause of the decline in fertility rates. In itself, the possibility of access to higher education is quite evidently an excellent thing. It is a concrete way of banishing discrimination and expressing the equal dignity of men and women. However, even though we should be happy over this development, we have to admit there is also an impact on fertility rates. Actually, the proportion of girls going for higher education is increasing everywhere: it is not rare for them to represent 50% of university students. Furthermore, as all the professors know, the female students do better at the universities than the boys. For these reasons—and without doubt for others—not only are they highly valued in the employment market, but they also appreciate the independence their salaries give them. Hence, they are not so eager to get married and have children.

4.   And that leads us to the following observation: the presence of women in the work force also makes fertility rates fall. First of all, there is no lack of employers who often discriminate against women who have children, "for they could have more." Some even exercise explicit pressure that their employees refrain from getting pregnant. Some managers even go so far as to require certificates of sterilization from prospective employees; even in Europe such cases have drawn attention. Moreover, maternity, which already compromises employment, also compromises the career of women. "If women have the opportunity of receiving the same education and the same possibilities of employment as men, but these possibilities are diminished if they have children, they will restrict the number of their children to such a point that, in the long run, their fertility will be greatly lessened."[1]

5.   The influence of mass communications, especially of TV, has profoundly altered the image of the family.[2] The respective roles of the man and the woman in marriage and society are changing: fidelity has become conditional and divorce has become commonplace. This influence creates conditions unfavorable to the transmission of life.

On four of the points we have just mentioned (2, 3, 4, 5) the influence of the ideology of *gender* is considerable and it is brought out very well in the monograph of Peter McDonald.[3]

6.   The influence of credit policies should also be pointed out. These facilitate access to certain kinds of consumer goods; as a consequence they tempt people to reduce the size of the family.[4] In effect, by facilitating access to credit for large segments of the population, the government opens easy access to consumption for these new borrowers. Now what do these new consumers buy? It is clearly seen that they prefer to acquire consumer goods like cars, costly TV sets or other products of comfort rather than invest in goods favorable to the family: schools, medical care, better prepared foods, etc.

7.   "The child is no longer what he was," one can say ironically. The child is the object of choice between him and other goods, among which he is not perceived as totally different. Other things are preferred to him: the house, the car, a computer, vacations, a dog, etc. He is no longer appreciated as the work of a couple whose future unfolds over a long period of time: conception, birth, education, training. Neither is the child seen as the one who is going to take on and carry the generational baton. He is frequently considered as an object to which one has a right, an object that one "files away"—in the crib, in a child-care facility—

while the parents work; that inclines some people to speak of "storage of the child."

8. The *transition from the "rural" to the "urban" life-style* is well-known for its effects on fertility rates. "Rural" life promotes solidarity among generations, a sense of responsibility and reciprocity. It favors the integration of private life with professional life. Small, medium or even large, the enterprise is a family affair in which each takes part. It is a setting of affective, professional, cultural and religious memory. Furthermore, in the countryside the child is considered from before adolescence as potential for work; he produces and contributes to the income of the family and its prosperity.

Migration to the towns and cities turns the individual in upon himself; the "rural" solidarities are no longer assured; awareness of individual rights is sharpened; the isolation, the tight quarters of his dwelling, the stress of employment, the spectre of unemployment are but a few of the factors that are conducive to having fewer children. The latter must most of the time await adulthood before being integrated into the work force.

9. Still other factors are mentioned by demographers, especially the experts brought together by the Population Division. One thinks particularly of a certain eugenic inclination displayed more and more which, for example, hunts down even before birth the infants with Down's syndrome. It is not an exaggeration to speak here of a rampant terrorism that has recourse to a wide range of effective means of "persuasion."

From age 35 on, or even before, women are pressured not to conceive, and if ever they violate this tacit order, they will be subjected to prenatal examinations accompanied by proposals close to coercion.[5] The child will no longer be allowed to live and to be born except with the reservation of a suspensive condition: he will have to be first approved as of irreproachable quality. Without that, in the name of the "rights of reproductive health," his mother will be allowed to "benefit" from a legal abortion.

10. The absence of a family policy, or worse policies that penalize couples who have children, have a dissuasive effect on young couples contemplating having children. The effect of these policies is nonetheless noticeable. Judicious measures can, for example, promote access to housing, adapt the educational system and improve health services. A good family policy produces positive effects which are easily observable. The measures taken in Sweden in order to revive a fertility rate in free fall were immediately followed by beneficial results—which, alas, ceased the moment these same measures were partially revoked.

The discriminatory and unjust fiscal regime to which married couples are subjected in many countries negatively affects fertility.[6] In Italy—champion in the fall of the birth rate—families of two children are subjected to a higher tax than those having only one. Is this a joke?

11. It also happens that a fraction of family allocations is transferred to budgets for social aid or even that these allocations are partially subject to taxation.

12. Let us emphasize again that couples of fertile age *fear the future*; they question the meaning of their existence. They worry about employment; in fact, the possibility of unemployment may even induce the young not to marry at all and, if they do marry, not to have children. Couples want to enjoy life but are afraid to transmit it. To transmit life always presupposes a lot of love as well as hope. This twofold motivation is often supplanted by fear.

ANTI-NATAL TECHNIQUES

All the anti-natal techniques have a direct negative impact on fertility.

"Provisional" Techniques

To impede the appearance of a child is, by definition, the objective of all contraceptive methods.[7]

Abortion kills the infant before its birth. That is why this infant is not counted in the infantile mortality rate. However, despite the sophisms of some demographers, babies thus eliminated constitute a demographic deficit.

From the strict descriptive viewpoint, contraception, abortion and the IUD have in common the fact that they do not definitively affect fertility. In effect, a woman can stop contracepting and have a baby; a woman who has had an abortion does not necessarily lose her ability to become a mother.

Definitive Techniques: *Infanticide and Sterilization*

Alongside provisional techniques, we should mention the definitive anti-birth techniques. We mention two.

• *Infanticide of females*

Besides abortion, which concerns the baby, there exists another more radical and definitive form of battle against fertility, and it envisages the woman: *infanticide of females*. In effect, since it is the woman who has the privilege of bringing new life to the world, some societies have decided to cut short this "risk" by killing little female babies. This particularly cruel practice is regularly reported in China where it creates considerable imbalance between the number of boys and girls. It suffices to measure and compare the bars or rectangles representing the 0 to 54 age brackets in the pyramid in China (cf. Illustration 7) to see that the number of men (on the left side of the pyramid) is constantly and obviously higher than that of women. This imbalance is especially flagrant for the age brackets 0 to 4 and 5 to 9 years. This is all the more astonishing in that the infant and juvenile mortality of boys is generally higher than that of girls. This practice leads to imbalances that Sylvie Brunel and Yves Blayo rightly call "stupefying." "In the province of Hainan, for example, there are 175 boys to 100 girls among women of fifty years old who have but one child."[8] Moreover, the results of wars, conflicts and accidents at work should appear in the shrinkage of the bars on the left side (men) in relation to those on the right (women). Yet the contrary is true.[9]

• *Sterilization*

The second, and in principle, definitive case is sterilization. Since it isn't as well known as contraception and abortion, we are going to take more time with it.

a) Today this practice is extremely widespread among poor populations. Very often local authorities offer this free "service" to ignorant women, mutilated forever, in conditions defying the most elementary principles of hygiene—and morality. Illustration 13 will give an idea of what presently happens. It has to do with women of a fertile age using whatever method possible to control birth. This illustration shows the staggering proportion of sterilized women.

ILLUSTRATION 13

Percentage of those having been sterilized

Region	Date Of The Data	Percent Sterilized	Source of the Data
World	1995	37	UNO
Brazil	1996	40.3	Government
Mexico	1995	43.3	Government

Source: For the world: *Informe conciso sobre la situación demográfica en el mundo en 1995* (New York: UNO, 1995) 21; for Brazil: *Pesquisa Nacional Sobre Demografia e Saúde 1996* (Brasilia: Ministério da Saúde and Rio de Janeiro: IBGE, 1997) 52 f.; for Mexico: *Programa Nacional de Población* (Mexico DF, Poder Ejecutivo Federal, 1995) 24.

This data is practically never reflected in the media. It is true that recently the media has denounced the assembly-line sterilizations that took place in Peru.[10] The same was done regarding countries where sterilizations were performed: China, Bangladesh,[11] Tibet and other parts of the world.

b) One frequently-asked question regarding these sterilizations is: are they performed with the consent of those concerned? The response reflects the variety of cases and situations. One thing is immediately plain to see: the women at whom the massive campaigns of sterilization are mostly aimed are poor women, often illiterate, whom paid doctors seduce into believing that the operation is "benign" and that it is "for their own good."

In fact, these sterilizations are always part of programs whose main motivation is corruption: corruption of the administrative personnel who "have to respect and make respected plans of public health"; corruption of the medical personnel who "have to attain the quotas assigned to them." In this latter case, they receive bonuses or compensation, for example a holiday. If they don't attain the fixed goals, they will be subject to penalties.[12] This corruption is often extended even to the victims themselves, since they are frequently given a pathetic tip for letting themselves be sterilized.[13]

c) It is expedient at this point to distinguish between *forced* and *coerced* sterilizations.[14]

• Forced sterilizations are those performed either by physical force or mental manipulation. In the first case, women are subjected to physical constraint and operated on. This practice has even been extended to men: in 1976 more than 6 million men were forcefully vasectomized in India. Deepra Dhanraï's film, *La guerre des naissances* (The Birth War) won an award in Nyon (Switzerland) in 1992 for having truthfully documented these campaigns which bring such shame to India , and are still going. In the case of mental manipulation, those responsible have recourse to lies: they deceive women about the nature, secondary effects and consequences of the operation and thereby obtain their consent.

By reason of the psychological vulnerability of poor women in the Third World, it should be recognized that forced sterilizations of the second type, that is by fraud or intellectual deception, are the most numerous. In Peru, it is precisely this practice which has recently been vigorously denounced.

The Example of Mexico

Mexico offers a particularly eloquent example of this sort of practice. According to a press release of the Zenit Agency, published on October 23, 1998, UNFPA had proposed to the Mexican government a remission of part of its debt on condition that these resources be used for demographic control, especially among young women in rural areas.

Actually, the medical personnel of Mexico have for many years had at their disposal a detailed manual explaining how to go about obtaining consent for sterilizing women. It couldn't be clearer that these types of sterilization are forced examples of the second type (mental manipulation). Moreover, the women—often deprived of any instruction—are invited to sign a declaration of "informed consent," unintelligible to the great majority of them. Illustration 14 reproduces the form.

ILLUSTRATION 14

Mexican Form of "Informed Consent"

INSTITUTO MEXICANO DEL SEGURO SOCIAL
DIRECCION DE PRESTACIONES MEDICAS
COORDINACION DE SALUD REPRODUCTIVA
Y MATERNO INFANTIL

Informed Consent

I understand that I have been provided with extensive information regarding the clear and precise benefits of using a method of contraception to take care of my health and to prevent pregnancies, for which I understand and I declare the following:

1. I have been informed that there exist temporary and permanent contraceptive methods for myself and my partner.

2. The temporary methods available in the IMSS are the oral contraceptives, intrauterine device (IUD) and contraceptive injections.

3. The permanent methods are: tubal ligation for women and the vasectomy for men.

4. The use of the permanent methods results in the inability to have children.

5. There are instances where both the temporary and the permanent methods may fail, and therefore the possibility of pregnancy exists.

6. I have been advised and informed of all the possible methods and the possible side-effects of each method.

7. That I have not been forced to respond to a medical exam in case of doubt or when indicated to me.

I have read the above and my decision is free, conscious and informed and I accept the use of the following method:

_____

I sign this consent of my free will and without any type of coercion in the presence of a witness that you chose.

_____
Signature and date

• There are three types of *coerced* sterilizations. First, there are the sterilizations to which women consent without having any real possibility of refusal. Such is the situation of women who, if they refused, would lose their job, or whose husband would lose his, or who would lose their housing, or who would pay heavy supplementary taxes, etc. Finally, coercive sterilizations are also those performed on women who are forced by hospital attendants into the operating room.[15]

---

[1] This is what Peter McDonald brings out in his "Gender Equity, Social Institutions and the Future of Fertility," *Demography*, Canberra, The Australian National University, Research School of Social Sciences, Working Papers, n. 69 (1997) 1. Here is the original English text: "If women are provided with opportunities near to equivalent to those of men in education and market employment, but these opportunities are severely curtailed by having children, then, on average, women will restrict the number of children that they have to an extent which leaves fertility at a precariously low, long-term level."

[2] G. Martine has emphasized the influence of this factor in Brazil. See *Brazil's Fertility.*

[3] We analyzed this ideology of *gender* in *The Gospel Confronting World Disorder* (St. Louis, MO: Central Bureau, 1999) 17-25. According to this ideology of gender, the division of roles of man and woman in society has no natural foundation; it is the product of culture and history.

[4] This factor plays an important role in Brazil as G. Martine demonstrates.

[5] On this matter see the points given toward the end of this chapter.

[6] Francis Bailleux, one of the best specialists of European fiscal law, has often touched on this problem. See especially "L'Etat du mariage toujours pénalisé," in *La Libre Belgique* (Brussels) financial supplement, March 28,1998) 25.

[7] One of the reference works that deals with the great demand for contraception, the technology it has put into play, the markets it has opened, the industrial enterprises interested in it, the changes in legislation it involves, etc., is that of Polly Harrison and Allan Rosenfield (eds.), *Contraceptive Research and Development: Looking to the Future* (Washington, D.C.: National Academy Press, 1996).

[8] See Sylvie Brunel and Yves Blayo, "La mort des petites filles chinoises," *Le Monde* (March 7, 1998).

[9] One begins to understand better the dramatic demographic situation in Russia. Contrary to the situation in China, in Russia we see a lack of *men*. Two great factors are responsible: First, the collapse of the fertility index. According to the *World Population Data Sheet* 1999 (Washington, D.C.: Population Reference Bureau), this index presently stands at 1.2. Secondly, a lowering of life expectancy at birth for *men* can be observed. This had been 63 in 1990; it is presently 57 (as opposed to 71 for women!). This is explained by Laure Mandeville in "La Russie sera le 'pays des veuves'," *Le Figaro* (Paris) July 2, 1999.

[10] Of articles published in Peru, see Arturo Salazar Larrain's "¿El exterminio de la población rural?" *El Comercio* (Lima) Feb. 23, 1998: "Silencio irresponsable," *ibid.*; "Ministro anuncia programa para evitar errores en planificación familiar" and "Piden informe sobre paciente que murió luego de vasectomía," *ibid.* April 2, 1998; "¿Quien responde por las campañas de esterilización y sus excesos?" *ibid.* April 3, 1998.

[11] On this case see Fenneke Reysoo, Anke van der Kwaak, Nasreen Huq, *The Incentive Trap. A Study on Coercion, Reproductive Rights and Women's Autonomy in Bangladesh* (Leiden: Rijks Universiteit, 1995).

[12] We offer a translation here of what F. Reysoo et al. wrote in *The Incentive Trap* about Bangladesh: "Besides the bonuses given to clients and to those who spur them on, some so-called dissuasive measures are aimed at the families of family planners. These dissuasive measures involve penalties for not attaining the goals assigned in the service [of birth control] of what concerns the new recipients and the number of those who escape. The providers of these services are liable to receive warnings or letters of dismissal" (24); see also 43 f.

[13] About this kind of corruption see F. Reysoo et al., *The Incentive Trap*, 21-24; 39-44; Appendix A on "Money in Exchange for Contraceptives?" (55-59) and Appendix B on "*The Corruption of Incentives*," (60 f.).

[14] This precise distinction is not used by many organizations defending the rights of man. It was clarified by the International Committee for Tibet whose seat is in San Francisco. In French it appears in a dossier published by Les Amis du Tibet under the title *Les Tibétaines privées du droit à la liberté de procréer* (Comines, Belgium, 1994). And we adopt this distinction here.

[15] On all this see *Les Tibétaines...* The prestigious review, *Cuadernos de Bioetica* (Santiago de Compostela), published an important dossier on this question entitled *Il consentimiento informado* in its 9th installment, n. 33,1, 1998.

CHAPTER III

CONSEQUENCES OF A DECLINE

The drop in fertility is a phenomenon that is certainly observable but relatively slow; people are thus less inclined to pay attention to it. The same holds true of the decline's consequences. And so we are going to examine some of the consequences and draw important lessons from them. Then we will delineate some comparisons.

1. First consequence: *the ageing of the population*. The median age is one which divides the population into two equal parts: for example, those who are at least 30 and those who are over 30. Around 1900 the median age of the world population was located at about 20. Presently in the developing countries it is around 25, while in the wealthy countries it is more on the order of 40. *The median age is rising everywhere.* According to a study published by the *Wall Street Journal*,[1] as 2025 approaches this median age would be 53 for Japan, 55 for Germany, 58 for Italy. Whence there arise questions which cannot be overlooked: how many women will there be in these countries of childbearing age; what will their level of fertility be?

Ageing as a signal would evidently be confirmed if we referred to the median age obtained by dividing the number of years lived by a population by the size of this same population. According to *Time*, in 1975 the median age of the world population was 22; in 2050 it could be 38.[2]

In certain cases this ageing attains dramatic proportions. According to the data of the Economic and Social Council of the UN, reproduced by the journal *ABC* (Madrid) of April 24, 1999, in 2050 the population of Spain will be the oldest in the world. For every person of less than 15 there will be 3.6 of sixty or older.

With reference to Italy, Jean-Claude Chesnais states: "The most extreme case is that of the central province, dense and rich, of Emilia-Romagna, whose chief city is Bologna and where the number of persons over 60 is twice that of youths younger than 20."[3] Peter McDonald makes the same observation: "In a stable population, with the level of fertility applicable in 1995 in Italy, the size of the population would fall in 100 years to only 14% of its initial level. The corresponding percentages would be respectively: for Spain 15%, for Germany 17%, for

Japan 28%. Even if it maintained its fertility index such as it was in 1995, that is, at the level of 1.7, the population of France in 100 years would fall to 50% of its initial level."[4]

Similar calculations had already been made in 1989 by Bourgeois-Pichat, who contemplated the "demographic implosion." The famous demographer had calculated that if the wealthy countries adopted the fertility norm which obtained at that time in the Federal Republic of Germany, the population of these countries would be extinguished by about 2250. With the same index applied to developing countries, their populations would disappear around 2400. This is shown in Illustration 15.

2. In its turn, ageing entails a direct consequence: *depopulation*. In effect, it is evident that the more men age the more probability there is that they will die. That is the reason why, as of now, the mortality rate is higher in wealthy countries than in the poor ones. In some wealthy countries in which fertility is dropping, depopulation is presently hidden by *more births*, a phenomenon familiar to demographers. Little known to the public at large, this phenomenon is nevertheless easy to understand and it is clearly seen in eastern Europe. In effect, in these countries, a number of infants die before reaching the age of 1, for hardly 70 years ago infant mortality was ten times higher than today. Furthermore, among those who survived, numerous are those who—especially due to war—have died before reaching the age one can hope for due to the present lengthening of life expectancy. All these "anticipated" deaths are, so to speak, forgotten, which gives a a *false* impression of more numerous births in relation to deaths. As a matter of fact, if all the people born in 1921 had lived to the age of 77 (actual life expectancy in wealthy countries), that is until 1998, deaths today would exceed births in these same countries. Besides, already in 15 European countries, among them Germany, the number of deaths surpass births.

3. Another consequence entailed by ageing, itself resulting from the drop in fertility: *the increase of the proportion of dependent elderly persons*. In the developed countries, the relationship between those who work and contribute and the retired who do not work is presently 3 to 1. If nothing changes, in 2030 this ratio will be 1.5 to 1. This phenomenon does not spare the developing countries. For the aged population to go from 7 to 14% of the total population in France a hundred years were

Illustration 15

The Scenario of the "Demographic Implosion"

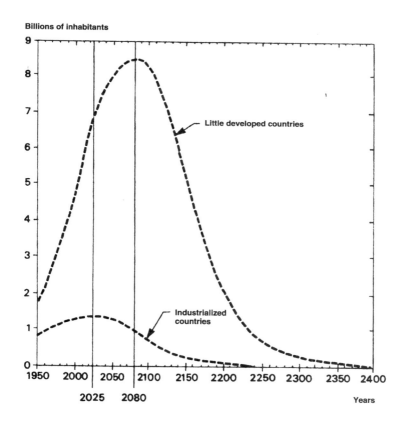

Billions of inhabitants

Source: Jean Bourgeois-Pichat, "Du XXe au XXIe siècle: l'Europe et sa population après l'an 2000," *Population* (Paris) Jan-Feb. 1989, p. 9-42; see p. 27; cited from F.G. Dumont, *Le monde et les hommes* (Paris: Litec, 1995) 33.

required; in China this same transition will last hardly 25 years.[5] The increase in the proportion of aged persons appears very clearly in the pyramids of ages. As an example we provide in Illustration 16 a pyramid of ages for Zurich.

Illustration 16

Zurich's Pyramid of Ages

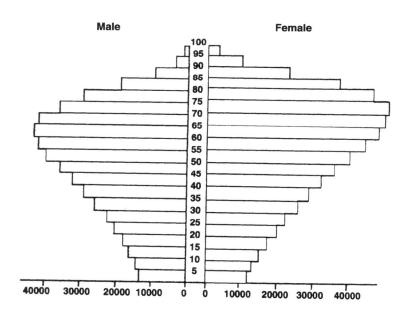

Source: François Geinoz (ed.) *Europe. L'Hiver démographique* (Lausanne: Ed. L'Age d'homme, 1989) 39.

4. *The foreseen collapse of the Social Security system* can be understood in the wide sense: family allocations, indemnities for unemployment, insurance, help for the handicapped, pensions for the disabled and aged, etc. To become more conscious of what is happening regarding pensions, let us invent a simplified example: in 1960, in such and such a country, the retirement age was fixed at 60 when one could expect to live till 67; the pension served for only 7 years then. In 1995, in this same country, the retirement age is fixed at 65 when one can hope to live till 79; hence the pension has to be available for 14 years, and for a population having growing medical needs.

Already sinister cracks can be seen in the organization of social aid. According to Peterson, who relied on official data, in thirty years the developed countries will have to devote between 9 and 16% of their GNP solely for honoring their commitments to pension matters.[6] At present, the regular increase of life expectancy cannot but aggravate these difficulties. In effect, the more people advance in age, the more they need health care. In turn, the latter becomes more and more costly especially due to the state of technology, ever-appealing to the field of medicine.

This collapse will be all the more aggravated by the way rich countries live above their means. In particular, they cling to social legislation voted in after the war, in a climate of prosperity, which today is no longer sustainable. Too many union agreements, for example, have become *conservative* by the very fact that, in their analysis, various systems don't take into account the problems issuing from the demographic evolution.

5. Besides, the Social Security budgets have already been quietly trimmed. However, these measures are shortsighted and totally insufficient; in fact, the days of State provision are necessarily numbered. We emphasize this soberly, for neither the legislatures, nor the policy makers in general, have the courage to tell citizens that the social advantages, in particular pension systems, are going to have to be revised downwards. On the contrary, they multiply reassuring assertions and promises that cannot be kept. Demographers and other specialists know perfectly well that radical reforms are imperative, indeed urgent. But the policy makers pretend to ignore their recommendations and in any case hardly take them into account. Long-term vision is alien: ostriches are in power. The more they procrastinate, the more unpopular will be the measures *which they will in any case have to take one day*.

39

From the political point of view, the future of democracy is in danger. Presently, to win elections, congressmen or MPs together with the political parties and governments bypass the problem by pretending that they have no choice: the voters demand above all that they preserve the social rights acquired in a context totally different from the current one. "Don't touch my acquired rights!" Undoubtedly; but this conservative and finally hypocritical conception of democracy compromises the very future of democracy and is an obstruction to any measure aimed at meeting the challenges that issue from the drop in fertility rates.

6. The *educational system* is also directly threatened. In industrialized countries, children up to the age of 20 are considered dependents. In practice, the number of young people effectively dependent embraces all the youth until the end of training or studies, and even up to the moment when they engage in a paying profession. Whatever may be the size of this group, it is added to the number of dependent aged persons, those over 64. In countries of the Third World, persons under 15 and over 64 are generally considered dependents.

Whence arise many, many difficulties in perspective. As for a lack in economic means, public powers are presently cutting back the educational budgets, while it is estimated that an aged person costs society twice that of a young person! Besides, since there are fewer children, courses must be eliminated, with evident repercussions on employment. Now all this happens at a time when youth are acquiring a volume of knowledge much more imposing and complex than what had to be assimilated by their parents. In effect, we must prepare youth for a greater productivity and above all for an enhanced creativity.

To that must be added—all other things being equal—that the discovery of promising talents, which, since schooling is obligatory, was made on a very large basis, that is for a great number of children, will henceforth be made on a more narrow base, with the inclusion of fewer children. One can immediately see the negative effect of this shrinkage at a time when we are all in accord in acknowledging that human capital and its formation carries much more weight than physical capital.[7]

7. Active adults are rapidly going to perceive the weight represented for them by the mass of aged dependent persons. For the former, this mass will be literally crushing, as shown by the age pyramids completely shaped like tops. It follows, then, that the adults, some of whom will be unemployed, will not indefinitely support the weight of these old people whose number will only increase.

This imbalance will result then in very strong tensions between the generations. These tensions will be further aggravated for two principal reasons. On the one hand, the active adults will have children; they will thus have the responsibility, not only of the dependent elderly of over 64, but also of a contingent of dependent young whose education they will have to ensure. On the other hand, these same adults will be reluctant to pay, by means of increased fiscal pressure, for the pensions and care of the elderly, while the latter, by reason of their electoral proportion, will "benefit" from the demagoguery of the politicians.

This "intergenerational" tension will be all the more radicalized to the degree that euthanasia is presented as the *final solution* to the impasse in Social Security.

8. A lower fertility entails a *weakening of memory*. This is a phenomenon often alluded to by Pierre Chaunu. In effect, culture is not transmitted first by books or computers. The bearers of culture are men who enrich it as they receive it. The arts, the crafts, the scientific disciplines are all going to become impoverished, yes, even disappear, because there will no longer be enough young people to receive them creatively.

The demographic implosion of industrialized countries is, therefore, a catastrophe for those countries having a rich cultural tradition, but it is also a catastrophe for the entire world. What gives these countries strength is precisely their capacity to create knowledge and *savoir-faire* in all fields. Observation also shows that their capacity is cumulative: it makes snowballs. Moreover, this capacity becomes concentrated. All the major discoveries of the twentieth century were made in the wealthy countries, even if they benefited from the support of the intellectuals originating in developing countries. If through human fault this creative capacity is lost, by virtue of the domino effect, the whole human community will suffer.

9. If children are lacking, customers also will eventually be lacking. Such is already the case for many industrial enterprises, especially those of a grand scale, for example in Germany. Some enterprises produce below their capacity for lack of enough customers. Once again it appears that unemployment has causes other than the increase in productivity.

One of these causes is the fact that factories are overextended due to lack of demand. In effect, it is not enough to increase productivity or to produce more than the market can absorb. Waste has its limits.

Corresponding to supply must, therefore, arise a like demand for the goods issuing from increased productivity. This demand cannot but come from a population which is itself growing.

Economic, agronomic, technological and industrial progress have thus favored acceptance of a more numerous population. This phenomenon is observable on a grand scale in contemporary India. In this country the green revolution was stimulated by Norman Borlaug, 1970 winner of the Nobel Peace Prize.[8] Less than forty years ago India counted some two hundred million inhabitants and was subject to terrible famines. Though all the problems are far from being resolved, India now counts nine hundred million people and *exports cereal*.

On the other hand, from the moment one has high productivity and an ageing population, the economic system is hit by dysfunction, for it does not make sense to strive to increase the supply of equipment and consumer goods when the demand is tending to weaken. This situation is made still worse by the fact that increasing productivity as a measure of reduction of production costs necessarily leads to unemployment and by that very fact contributes toward lessening demand.

10. Development requires investment. . . no one can invest by indefinitely having recourse to loans. In order to be able to invest, the economy must generate surpluses. That means saving is necessary to make investment possible. Consequently, the capacity to produce must always be higher than the mere ability of taking care of needs. In other words, the economy must not simply satisfy needs; it must also produce savings.

It is this context of the ageing of the population which gives rise to a most fearsome peril for many countries. In effect, an ageing population, that is, one in which a large proportion of dependent elderly people is concentrated, tends to produce less, invest less and consume savings. An ageing population tends to put a brake on investment of productivity and capacity; nor does it lend itself to creativity. It tends, therefore, not only to consume savings, but to have recourse to loans whose weight is transferred to the shoulders of the next generation. It could also happen that, through a reversal of the situation, the ageing countries are brought to the point of borrowing from emerging nations that have become capable of producing surplus and exportable capital.[9] The hour may sound for the shepherdess, formerly "helped" by the shepherd, to reverse the roles, and become the leader rather than the debtor, and perhaps even subject the former shepherd to one-sided conditions.

These traps are all the more dangerous insofar as they are hardly perceived. They are further aggravated by fiscal policies. It may happen that savings would be used as means of employment, modernizing instruments of production and infrastructure. But current fiscal policies discourage savings and sometimes penalize them by turning the investing potential represented by the savings toward social ends. How does this diversion work? Due to the pressure of an ageing population, fiscal policies are elaborated to serve the artificial protection of social policies (early pensions, retirement, insurance, unemployment, etc.). We say artificial protection, because the population can no longer permit itself such liberalities due to an age structure in which the elderly predominate.

In this connection, a young and growing population would bring about considerable advantages, for such a population exercises a favorable pressure on investments, productivity and creativity. A growing population will lead to production, then, not only in order to satisfy needs, but also to generate savings to invest. As we have already seen, in order for a country to develop, it cannot indefinitely have recourse to loans.

Here again appears the fatal error of ageing wealthy nations: they have not properly evaluated the importance of human capital in the contemporary economy. With all due respect, they fail to understand that a population functions rather like a machine. In a factory, one doesn't replace twenty year-old machines with new machines of the same model. Old machines must be replaced with machines that are more productive. Likewise, a given population must be replaced by a more productive one, that is, better prepared and more effective. This is what is required of family and educational policies which do not voluntarily support the elderly.

The youth of a population, then, offers a major comparative advantage to developing countries, on condition that these countries are not crushed by nonsensical debts, and that they are not prevented in practical terms from developing all the potential of their human capital.

11. We are now going to explain a consequence that is undoubtedly less well-known: it is, however, along with the preceding, one of the most grave. It concerns *violent imbalances* that can be foreseen in the *age structures* observed in different countries or groups of countries. Just as there will soon be in wealthy countries,[10] there will also be, in an analogous fashion, tensions among nations or regions[11] in which fertility is characterized by differentials, that is, by gaps accentuated and reflected in the age structure. These tensions will be all the more formidable in that the different nations or regions are all ageing, but at different paces.

We must not imagine that the South, demographically more dynamic, will display a more attentive solidarity toward the senile North. Nor must we wait for the "younger" nations of the European Union to fly to the help of "aged nations." A remark made by Amartya Sen regarding unemployment in the European Union deserves mention at this point:

> A single currency [writes the winner of the 1998 Nobel Prize in Economics] appreciably reduces the field of maneuverability of governments when they must face up to problems like unemployment or recession. They lack the tool of adjustment that rates of exchange provided, [...] Those responsible (the European Central Bank) see as their principal task to assure "monetary stability." They favor low inflation over low unemployment. The principal difference between Europe and the United States is that in terms of priority the US is more interested in the reduction of unemployment.[12]

If the field of maneuverability is reduced when faced with unemployment, it will be all the more so when faced with the consequences of a decline in fertility. Given the rigidity of the European monetary system, the member nations, with their economic differences, will have much trouble in determining measures adjusted to the state of their respective populations. This situation is, then, a cause of tension within the European Union itself.

12. The pressure of the migration of young populations coming from the so-called countries of the South will become increasingly stronger, and no regulation will succeed in containing it. Already evident in France, Italy and the United States, this pressure of migration will undoubtedly be one of the great challenges of the twenty-first century. Around the year 2030, 30% of the population of Germany will be comprised of foreigners. In Munich and Frankfurt, this percentage will surpass 50%![13] These migratory tides will not fail to have profound repercussions on the political life of each nation and on international relations.

13. The drop in fertility and, as a corollary, the imbalance in age structures, will also entail very serious consequences in international relations.

This is due first to the total number and age structure of the population's bearing on the affirmation of a given nation's sovereignty in the general context of international relations. History demonstrates this phenomenon, and present experience confirms it. The state of a nation's population certainly does not suffice for the political strength of a country, but it is one of the clear and necessary components. Gerard-François Dumont has devoted seminal studies to this problem.[14] As an example, he remarks that despite their ideological differences, no great Western nation "can allow itself to entertain a bad relationship with China." And the Sorbonne professor adds that, if General Pinochet had been leader of a country more important than Chile (15 million inhabitants), "his fate would have been different."

Next, the size and age structure of a population bear on defenses of a nation faced with external threats. The war in Serbia should be revealing here, especially for Europe. The latter is finally beginning to question its own system of defense and its crucial dependence upon the United States in this regard. Peterson, whom we are closely following, rightly observes that the developed but ageing countries will have to begin important investments for their own defense.[15] At present, the costs of an effective defense are steady: they must respond to external threats. But in a demographically ageing nation these costs must be distributed among a population that is shrinking and ageing and, moreover, whose revenues are tending to diminish. Furthermore, as we have already pointed out with regard to education (n.6), the ageing population is going to pressure governments into trimming defense budgets in order to protect social acquisitions. Now these acquired social goods include not only pensions, but also medical services. And so one can foresee that the ageing electorate will prefer to increase the budget for state-of-the-art medical technology and/or prolonging life expectancy to the detriment of state-of-the-art armaments. The need for the latter is caused, not only by threats with which the given country had to be able to cope, but also by reason of the diminishing number of young people. And thus we arrive at a vicious circle!

14. To understand and visualize all of this, one has first to refer back to Illustrations 4, 5, 6, 7 and 16. One should compare those pyramids with those of the countries which we are going to present, namely, those which are more or less committed to development.

Essentially, one will notice two things: first of all, even in these countries there is a tendency toward a drop in fertility; but above all, the level of the young proportion of the population is striking. Compared to the following illustrations which have the shape of a fir tree, Illustrations 4, 5, 6, 7 and 16 have an inverse look, the form of a top or mushroom. Here are Illustrations 17, 18, 19 and 20.

Illustration 17

Age Pyramids for Algeria

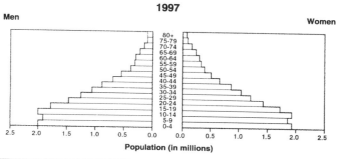

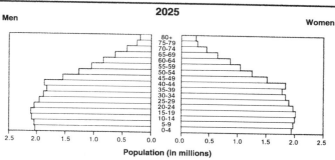

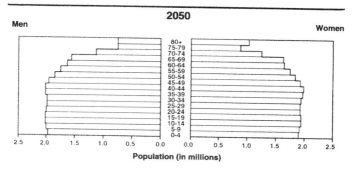

Source: Census Bureau, Washington, D.C., 1999

Illustration 18

Age Pyramids for Morocco

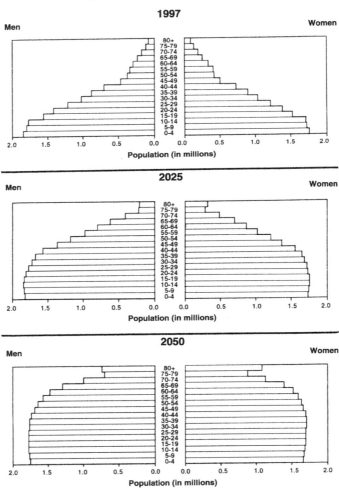

Source: Census Bureau, Washington, D.C., 1999

Illustration 19

Age Pyramids for Iran

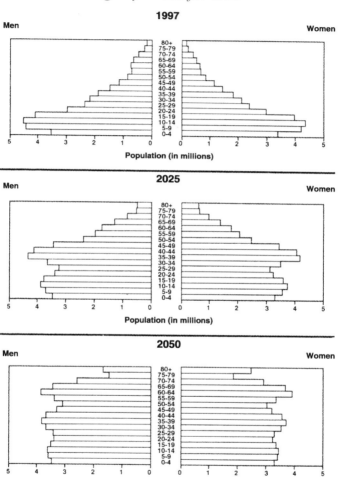

Source: Census Bureau, Washington, D.C., 1999

Illustration 20

Age Pyramids for Turkey

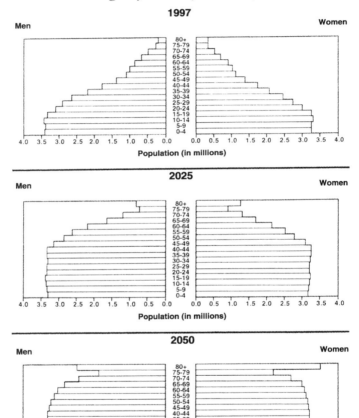

Source: Census Bureau, Washington, D.C., 1999

To recapitulate, Illustration 21 indicated in thousands the number of inhabitants estimated for the various countries we have cited, to which we add Germany. One can see that between 1997 and 2050 the estimate of the median rate of increase is lower nearly everywhere compared to the rate of increase indicated by the Population Reference Bureau for 1999. Two exceptions are shown in italics in the table: the USA and Iran.

Illustration 21

Population in 1997 and 2050 (in thousands)

Country	Population 1997 (in thousands)	Population 2050 (in thousands)	Growth Rate (1997-2050)	Avg. Annual Growth Rate (1997-2050)	Natural Growth Rate in 1999
France	58.609	48.219	− 18%	− 0,34	0,3
Spain	39.108	29.405	− 25%	− 0,47	0,0
Italy	56.831	38.290	− 33%	−0,62	− 0,0
Germany	82.072	57.429	− 30%	−0,57	− 0,1
China	1.226.275	1.332.435	+ 9%	0,17	1,0
Mexico	96.807	167.479	+ 73%	1,38	2,2
Brazil	167.661	228.145	+ 36%	0,68	1,5
USA	267.901	394.241	+ 47%	*0,89*	0,6
Algeria	29.830	58.880	+ 97%	1,83	2,4
Morocco	28.565	52.069	+ 82%	1,55	1,7
Iran	67.540	142.336	+ 111%	*2,09*	1,8
Turkey	63.528	103.649	+ 63%	1,19	1,5

Source: Census Bureau, 1998, and *World Population Data Sheet*, published by the Population Reference Bureau, Washington, 1999.

---

[1] "The Population Implosion," in the *Wall Street Journal* of October 16, 1997, distributed by Family of the Americas, e.mail: Family@upbeat.com.15 Cf. Peterson, "Gray Dawn," fol. 6.

[2] "Gray Matters: Malthus was Wrong," *Time* (April 19, 1999).

[3] Jean-Claude Chesnais, *Le crépuscule de l'Occident. Dénatalité, conditions des femmes et migrations* (Paris: Laffont, 1995) 61.14 In particular see his article, "Démographie et analyse stratégique," *Défense* [Paris] 83 (March 1999) 76-80.

[4] Peter McDonald, *Gender Equity*, 1 f.

[5] According to P. Peterson, "Gray Dawn," fol. 2.

[6] *Ibid.* fol 3.

[7] On this subject see the noted work of G. Becker, *A Treatise on the Family*, 13. According to Peterson in "Gray Dawn," fol. 2.

[8] See Gregg Easterbrook, "Forgotten Benefactor of Humanity," *The Atlantic Monthly* January 1977, 75-82.12 Amartya Sen, "L'Europe va réduire les marges de manoeuvre," interview in *Libération* (Paris) Oct. 19, 1998. Sen developed his ideas in *L'Economie est une science morale* (Paris: La Découverte, 1999).

[9] This case is envisioned by P. Peterson, "Gray Dawn," fol. 4.

[10] See note 7.

[11] Cf. Gérard-François Dumont, *Les spécificités démographiques des régions et l'aménagement du territoire* (Paris: Ed. des Journaux officiels, 1996).

[12] Amartya Sen, "L'Europe va réduire les marges de manoeuvre," interview in *Libération* (Paris) Oct. 19, 1998. Sen developed his ideas in *L'Economie est une science morale* (Paris: La Découverte, 1999).

[13] According to Peterson in "Gray Dawn," fol. 2.

[14] In particular see his article, "Démographie et analyse stratégique," *Défense* [Paris] 83 (March 1999) 76-80.

[15] Cf. Peterson, "Gray Dawn," fol. 6.

CHAPTER IV

THE UN AND ITS POPULATION CONFERENCES

Introduction

When one speaks of respect for life and defense of the family, it is frequently inferred, especially in Catholic milieux, that it is a question of an ethical, sexual or conjugal problem; thus, it would concern an essentially "private" moral problem. Clearly this perception is perfectly valid; it is even indispensable. However, it is fundamentally incomplete. To respect life and the family is equally a *social and political* ethical question that concerns *nations, their sovereignty and their populations,* especially those that are most vulnerable. This question also concerns *relations among nations.*

Today, by reason of its effect on persons and families, this political dimension of the respect for life and the family is, in a certain way, more important than the private dimension. The lack of respect by public authorities for life and for the family compromises the future of nations. We must, then, be aware of the impact exercised by policies that make little of life, the family, and entire segments of the world population. The present chapter will set the international dimension of these policies in particular relief.

HISTORICAL ORIGINS OF POPULATION POLICIES

The Ideological Components

Three major ideological sources are at the root of present demographic policies.[1]

1. *Malthusian Theses.* Malthus (1766-1834), an Anglican pastor, claimed that population growth was more rapid than the increase in food sources. This thesis is repeated to this day, but discredited by facts. If Malthus had been right, the world population would not have been able to surpass 900 million inhabitants at the beginning of the 19th century to the approximately six billion which it is at present. As a good economist imbued with liberal ideology, Malthus recommended that the poor not be helped: according to him, one had to allow natural selection to operate, which would eliminate them and limit their proliferation. He also advocated late marriages.

Going further, Francis Galton (1822-1911) recommended *artificial* selection: by having recourse to medical intervention, society must encourage the transmission of life among the rich, whose wealth attests to their superior genetic endowment, and restrain the transmission of life among the poor, whose very poverty manifests their pitiful genetic quality.

2. *Neomalthusian theses*, developed particularly by Margaret Sanger (1883-1966) and Marie Stopes, combine those of Malthus and Galton with *hedonist* theses—which assert the right to maximum individual pleasure—and *utilitarian* theses.[2] According to this ideology, one's "partner" is "interesting" to the degree in which he brings pleasure or profit. As a consequence, the neomalthusians preach free love, contraception, the rejection of marriage, racism and eugenics.

3. *Ecological theses.* These go back to the Nazi idea of living space which is sometimes presented as "sphere of influence," "garden," "frontier," "hunting reserves," etc. These theses maintain that because of the increase in the poor populations and their ignorance, they badly manage natural resources, that they lack responsibility, that they degrade the surrounding milieu, etc. The human population must be confined within the limits of "sustainable," or "lasting" development. "Mother Earth" must be respected: the New Age ideology shows its true colors here as well.

The three ideological components we've just pointed out are going to inspire conduct which is variously reflected in private practices (of individuals: libertinism, license, etc.) as well as public practices (of public authorities). It is these last that we are now going to consider.

FROM IDEOLOGY TO PRACTICE

Together or individually, these three ideological components are constantly invoked today to "justify" and "legitimize" control of life, the family, population, especially in countries of the South.[3] We are going to mention a few examples of personalities or institutions which, in the middle of the twentieth century, have recommended putting these theories into practice.

Already in 1921, Marie Stopes founded in England the first birth control clinic in a poor quarter. Another pioneer was Frank Notenstein who, in 1944, suggested the inclusion of birth control in public health programs. Notenstein became the first head of the Population Commission of the UN, founded in 1945. In 1946 a notorious eugenicist was named president of the then recently-founded UNESCO, namely, Julian Huxley. Margaret Sanger, already cited, founded in 1948 what would become the International Planned Parenthood Federation (IPPF), which claims 140 subsidiaries throughout the world. In 1952 John D. Rockefeller, Jr. founded the Population Council, the direction of which was entrusted to another militant eugenicist, Frederick Osborne.

Later, in the *Meadows Report* (1972), the Club of Rome predicted that growth has its limits. The Malthusian theses were crossed with those relating to living space. Thus arrived the order of ideas asserted by Maurice King in 1990: the poor were a threat to the surrounding environment. As a consequence, he advised that we let them die in the event that the campaigns of demographic control failed.

In the directly political domain, we should recall that after the Second World War the United States and other wealthy countries demographically less populated and having few primary resources, did not hide their distrust at the increase of poor populations. In this regard, William Draper's interventions were very explicit. This North American colonel claimed that the developing countries having significant resources were in need of the supervision of *rangers* (1971)! Since then Paul and Anne Ehrlich have made a fortune by "scientifically" asserting that living space was threatened by demographic growth and that, without radical measures, "we are heading toward a certain death."[4]

In order not to prolong this list, let us simply mention Zbigniew Brzezinski,[5] who in 1969 turned the East-West antagonism into a North (rich)-South (poor) one. Let us also mention Robert McNamara,[6] who opened wide the doors of the UN, especially those of the World Bank, to the anti-population ideologies. Finally, we should cite Henry Kissinger,[7] who in 1974 had a terrible report prepared. A reading of this report is indispensable, and its title could not be more explicit: "Implications of the growth of world population for the security of the United States and its overseas interests."

The First International Population Conferences

The first international conferences on population were devoted more to technical questions about demography. We will limit ourselves here to mentioning the main meetings organized by the UN.[8]

The *first conference* took place in Rome in 1954. It is of special interest to us, for it declared that decisions relative to the fertility of each person constituted a fundamental human right.

During the *second conference* (Belgrade 1965) it was observed that the United States wanted to insert birth control as an "aid" to development. In addition, the right of individuals to determine their fertility was inserted into a social and international context.

These themes were taken up again with more force by the wealthy countries with the *third conference* that was held in Bucharest in 1974. Followed by the rich countries, until then reserved, the United States tried to impose the idea that population growth—as it happens in the Third World—was an international problem. Whence the need to reinforce "aid" in this regard and the necessity of determining a plan of action. The poor countries reacted vigorously when faced with this reading of the situation and the projects of more effective demographic control. The members of the Group of 77 then launched their famous slogan: "The best contraceptive is development."

It was in Mexico City in 1984 that the *Fourth Conference of the United Nations on Population* was held. Drawing lessons from Bucharest, the conference wanted to decide on a plan of action for stabilizing world population. The United States manifested the determination to take the leadership in the action of the UN. However, President Reagan vetoed abortion as a means of birth control.

Above all we should remember that, according to the schema of demographic change,[9] a schema mostly ignored by the international conferences, the median birth rate of world population has been falling since the end of the sixties.

From Rome to Mexico, we can note, then, a magnification of the problem of population. In Rome it was a matter of experts meeting; at Belgrade demography was brought into relationship with political and economic questions; at Bucharest it was asserted that population was tied to the surrounding environment and to international questions. At Mexico City a plan of action was made more precise.

We will immediately see that the more recent conferences have increasingly radicalized the problem at the same time as they integrated it within other parameters.

THE MAJOR CONFERENCES OF THE 1990s

Now we are going to review the main international meetings that dealt with the question of population. Our review will not only be chronological, but also thematic.

Rio, 1992: The First Summit about the Earth and the Environment

Inaugurating a practice which would become standard, this conference at Rio consisted of two parallel meetings: the official meeting, that is, of heads of State or government, and the gathering of non-governmental organizations (NGOs).

A) From the official meeting, that of the heads of government, there issued a declaration, two conventions (on the atmosphere and biodiversity) and *Agenda 21*. This Agenda drew the lines of action aimed at reconciling development with the environment. Behind the official rhetoric which presented the earth as "our common house" the real aims clearly appeared. It was a matter, for the more wealthy countries, to defend what they considered their "vital space": the sources of raw materials that are abundant in the poor countries, which—they say—irrationally exploit them, waste them and pollute the environment. What is in play here is the project for withdrawing control from poor countries over their own natural resources. In summary, it is a question of limiting their sovereignty. Between the lines read particularly the internationalization of the Amazon basin.

B) In parallel fashion the *Global Forum* of the nongovernmental organizations was unfolding; therein figured Greenpeace, Cousteau, Raoni and other media celebrities. New Age themes relative to Mother Earth were propagated; homosexual personalities were on display. Signed by well-known learned persons the "Heidelberg Call" was distributed. Not content to invoke the so-called "plague of overpopulation," these learned people insisted on the non-polluting character of scientific progress and technological applications derived from it. More subsidies, please!

Vienna, 1993: Human Rights

This conference invited us to fix our attention on the trap of consensus. The organizers of these international conferences boast of arriving at decisions by consensus. Nonetheless, this consensus frequently skirts around discordant voices. In its Chapter II, art.5, the final Declaration states:

> The world conference on the rights of man encourages States to consider limiting the impact of the reservations they expressed in regard to the international instruments concerning this matter [namely, human rights], to formulate all the reservations with as much precision and circumspection as possible, to see to it that none is incompatible with the object and purpose of the treaty in question, and to examine regularly the reservations already formulated with a view to withdrawing them.

Evidently, this recommendation has the objective of seeing that the "consensual decision" adopted in the international meetings prevails over national laws. For example, if the "plan of action" adopted in an international conference involves a program for "stabilizing the population" or of "reproductive health," everything that is not in harmony with such a program will have to be withdrawn from national legislation. The conventions will furnish the appropriate juridical instruments to repeal national laws.

Cairo, 1994: Population and Development

Prepared for by the various previous meetings, the Cairo "Summit" unfolded also on a twofold level. The official conference brought together some 10,000 delegates; the nongovernmental organizations assembled the representatives of about 500 organizations. We will focus our attention on the official conference.

Since—according to the version of the organizers—poverty is the consequence of demographic growth, the objective of the meeting was the approval of a plan of action over twenty years to control the world population,[10] the inference being that it must be stabilized. Taking account of this goal, one recommended "reproductive health"; this includes—incontestably—the anticonceptive panoply. Little interest was shown in marriage and maternity, but various other forms of union were envisioned. Control of population requires the cooperation of the woman whose socioeconomic status must be improved: even the education of women was slipped in among the means of limiting births!

58

After a very lively discussion and forceful pressure on the part of the Holy See's delegation, and those of various Catholic and Muslim countries, the final document states that "in no case can abortion be promoted as a means of contraception."[11]

Unfortunately, while they adequately discussed the means for controlling population, they hardly disputed the basis of the problem: the hypothetical validity of the conference's objective, that is, the timeliness of a twenty-year plan of action aimed at containing the growth of the world population. Since the Cairo Conference, this plan has constantly been invoked in subsequent international conferences, and it has been put into practice, notably in its financial aspect.[12]

In this conference, the decisive role was played by the large delegation of the United States as well as by the servile delegations of the European Union and Japan. Not less decisive was the action of the IPPF, as active through its delegation as through their agents who had been installed in key posts in the official meeting.[13]

Copenhagen, 1995: Social Development

Less popularized by the media than the others, this meeting (March 6-12) was devoted to social development. This conference recommended the creation of employment to fight against poverty. Two points were raised which are of particular interest to us because they are consistent with the dynamic of the other meetings. First, the conference recommended the integration of those who engage in conduct outside the norm: sexual matters are understood here. Secondly, one observed the involvement of the nongovernmental organizations on a far larger scale than in the other meetings.

Beijing, 1995: Woman

Once again to meetings.

1. The Fourth Conference of the UN about Women took place in the Chinese capital from September 4 to 15. The United States and the delegation—always so servile—of the European Union once again voiced their refrain about "reproductive rights." These same delegations took the occasion to push the theme "liberty to decide" in the matter of abortion. All the themes of radical feminism were addressed at the meeting. The theme of "gender" was omnipresent. According to the latter, differences between the sexes really don't matter; the diverse roles attributed by society to men and women have, not a natural, but a cultural origin. Society invented the diverse roles to oppress women. On the basis of that, it is clear, that they contest and devalue monogamous marriage founded on heterosexual union, maternity that flows from such union, and the family that is the fruit of this union.[14] For good measure, the delegations wanted to make commonplace and normalize the "new models" of union: homosexual, lesbian, single parent, male or female, etc.

The ideology of "gender" entails another consequence: The erosion of the rights and duties of parents in the education of their children. In particular, adolescents have to enjoy a broad sexual freedom withdrawn from interference by their parents and accompanied by the "services" required by this explicit incitement to license. "Sexual education" is conceived here as an encouragement to sexual indulgence, to contraception, to abortion.

Very curiously, the conference remains very discreet about the exploitation of women in pornography and prostitution.

2. The Forum of the nongovernmental organizations at Huariou (North of Beijing), from August 30 to September 8th, assembled the upper crust of radical feminism and provided the participants of the official meeting with their ideological results (which, in any case, were not lacking). The members of the Forum intervened throughout the Beijing Conference as both pressure group and lobby. Since this happened continually, the IPPF played the principal role here. One should also note, however, the "message" of the Ford Foundation: it is advisable to work on the public and to change people's mentality in order to bring about new public and private attitudes favorable to demographic control.[15]

Istanbul, 1996: Housing

This meeting (June 3-14) was not to have the same importance as the big meetings which preceded it. It was supposed to have the goal of verifying the application of the accords reached—they claim—by "consensus" at Rio, Cairo and Beijing.[16] Have governments respected the guidelines established by the plans of action? It seems that the response had not been as affirmative as they could have hoped.

Population control was decidedly not forgotten: the question of land management, urban concentration and housing implied a change of mentality (already recommended at Beijing). Families would have to have access to smaller social housing that would force them to have fewer children. The Beijing theme of the "polymorphous family" was made more precise: Those same rights recognized for the traditional monogamous families would also have to be recognized for homosexuals and lesbians. Among these figures the right to adopt.

Moreover, the theme of the environment, taken up at Rio (1992), was highlighted anew. Mother Earth would suffer from too many human beings. It no longer suffices simply to respect Gaia; we must render her a cult: man and humanity must be subject to her.

Another Beijing theme also resurfaced: that of removing parental responsibility for the education of their children. A consequence of "gender" is that woman, following the example of man, must produce. Hence, society must have the competence to educate children, including in matters of sexuality.

Finally, at Istanbul, the power of the nongovernmental organizations was confirmed. The organizations present were chosen with care: none was retained that did not prove its determination to cooperate unreservedly with the programs of action. Moreover, these nongovernmental organizations were not limited to merely observing: they participated in the working meetings and in the formulation of documents.

Rome, 1996: Food Security

In the course of the different conferences which we have reviewed, the influence of pro-life groups and family movements—although still too few—had grown. We see among them an acute realization of the stakes; these groups improved their organization, making them more effective.

Aware of this fact, the technocrats of the UN were unexpectedly obliged to highlight the meeting of the UN Fund for Nutrition, which was held in Rome from November 13th to the 17th. This in no way indicated a significant improvement of the rhetoric of earlier meetings. Rather, what was reaffirmed was the endless Malthusian thesis: the "food security" of a good part of humanity (read the poor) is threatened due to an excess in population. It was considered urgent, then, to make extraordinary efforts in various fields to contain population: sexual education, training of women, reproductive health, the environment, etc. Furthermore, the wealthy countries proclaimed their firm intention to work in all sectors where such population control must be exercised. This intention was clearly announced in particular by a delegate of the

United States. The US would be disposed to stop "aid" and even use food as a weapon, if the poor countries, considered as "overpopulated," would not feel obliged to accept control programs so generously offered by those who know the roads to prosperity. . .

The Conferences of 1997

Various events that are of interest to us came about in the course of 1997.

1. The meeting of G8 in Denver, bringing together the heads of State of the more wealthy countries, ended on June 22nd. Some flagrant differences of opinion became apparent between the European Union and the United States regarding various points, in particular, regarding carbon dioxide emissions and the greenhouse effect. The United States—in a flagrant abuse of its dominant position—refused all concessions. Also in the matter of unemployment, the United States wished to employ merciless neoliberal methods, while the European Union announced its desire to solve this problem with a marked social preoccupation.

Denver made clear the relative isolation of the United States and allowed the European participants to see just how much of a distance separated them from the USA. For the European Union, Denver was both a source of irritation as well as an occasion of a salutary awakening. To the degree that it refused ideological and political connivance with the United States, it became evident that the European Union could, if it wanted to, recover some of its credibility before the Third World. The basic condition of this recovery was the fidelity of Europe to its ideals of liberty, and also of justice and solidarity. For example, the problem of unemployment that afflicts the European Union cannot be resolved to the detriment of the poor countries.

2. The Rio de Janeiro meetings (March 13-21, 1997) had the objective of preparing the second Earth Summit which was to take place in June in New York (cf. n. 3 below). There were two associated meetings of nongovernmental organizations: radical feminists and ecologists. Despite the nongovernmental character of these meetings, high UN functionaries attended them. The president of Brazil himself, Fernando Henrique Cardoso, as well as the prefect of Rio de Janeiro, enhanced these meetings with their presence. They dealt with examining whether Agenda 21 of the 1992 Summit had been respected.

a) Hotel Gloria was the locale for the eighth international conference on Woman and Health. During the meeting, the themes which were habitually addressed at similar conclaves were again discussed. As on other similar occasions, the Catholic Church was the object of those same attacks generally reserved for her. The participants also recommended that public aid for development be channeled through the nongovernmental organization. At the end of the conference the *Gloria Declaration* was supposed to be made public.

b) The Sheraton Hotel was the locale for the meeting of the Earth Council which was attended by personalities such as Mikhail Gorbachev, Mercedes Sosa, Paulo Freire, Frederico Mayor (Director General of UNESCO), Maurice Strong (of the General Secretariat of the UN), James Wolfenshohn (president of the World Bank), observers from UNICEF, of the UNPD, UNFPA, etc. Curious, isn't it, a meeting of nongovernmental organizations, and imprudent on the part of high international functionaries!

The objective of this meeting was the preparation of the Earth Charter, which was intended to become a "universal code of conduct" outweighing the Universal Declaration of the Rights of Man of 1948. It aimed at rejecting the Ten Commandments and at deposing the traditional anthropology.[17] Henceforth, man would no longer be king of nature; he is just some parcel of it. Anthropocentrism has had its day: man becomes a particle in a pantheistic cosmology, according to the better style of the New Age. Even its vocabulary banishes the expression "dignity of man" because its connotation was judged to be too Christian. According to Gorbachev—who, it was whispered, let himself be bought—this charter traces the axes of the "global government": a program that the UN should launch.

3. The second Earth Summit, known as "Rio+5," was held in New York from June 23-27, 1997. A hundred and seventy delegations attended in the presence of numerous heads of State. There was unanimity about one thing: this meeting was a resounding failure. The participants could not even produce a final declaration; it was impossible to reach a consensus, always so ardently desired. Those who saw in this meeting "the death certificate of the Rio spirit" were not without reason.

Moreover, a sign of hope was observed: namely, the sovereign freedom with which the leaders of the Group of 77 as well as developing countries in general expressed themselves with regard to the topic of sensitivity toward the poor. Such, for example, was the case of the Summit's president, Razali Ismail (of Malaysia), and of president Mkapa of Tanzania. Despite the propaganda of earlier meetings, the Gloria Declaration, the Earth Charter, etc., the concept of "enduring development," in its Malthusian version, had a decidedly difficult time being universally accepted.

Activities of 1998

During the year 1998, innumerable initiatives were commenced. Let us note in passing that they attested to the inexhaustible character of the financial resources at the disposal of the international organizations revolving within the orbit of the UN. We will mention only a few of these initiatives.

1. A session of ECLAC (Economic Commission for Latin America and the Caribbean [of the UN]) merits attention with a little detail. It took place from May 11 to 16 in Oranjestad (Aruba) and was devoted to the themes "Population, Reproductive Health and Poverty." More precisely, it was a matter of verifying the implementation of and effects produced by the Consenso Latinoamericano del Caribe sobre Poblacion y Dearrollo (Latin American Consensus on Population and Development), a regional document of 1993 in preparation for Cairo (1994); Cairo's Program of Action; the Regional Plan of Action prepared by the Secretariat of CEPAL in 1996, a document applying Cairo's Program of Action.[18]

It was a question of preparing, on these foundations, various round tables, seminars and other symposia, organized beginning with the second semester of 1998 by UNFPA in view of two important conferences in 1999.

2. The foundation of the International Criminal Court was decided in Rome on July 18. This was to have the task of judging cases of genocide and crimes against humanity. In order to avoid being called before the International Criminal Court, States would have to incorporate the "new rights of man" into their legislation.[19]

According to the *New American* magazine (Appleton, WI) of August 31, the creation of this International Criminal Court is seen as a major victory by the World Federalist Movement. This movement gathers together the nongovernmental organizations supporting "globalism," "one world approach," that is more explicitly the idea of one single world government.[20] For a long time this movement has been financed by the Ford, Rockefeller, Carnegie and MacArthur foundations, by the UN, the European Commission and the Council of Foreign Relations. This current aims at checking the sovereignty of people, and then States, and from there to deprive States of all right to control international organizations.[21]

Hence, it isn't surprising that some State members had closely observed the nongovernmental organizations' "No Peace Without Justice (NPWJ)," which was a campaign aimed at the earliest possible ratification of the decision to create the Court.[22]

3. From August 4th to the 9th of 1998, a conference was held in Lisbon, assembling a hundred or so *ministers representing youth.* During this meeting the discussions on the meaning of words like "family" and "health" were taken up again. *The Declaration of Lisbon on Youth* includes above all the rejection of any reference to the responsibility of parents in sexual matters. According to the interpretation of some, from the age of 10 onward (!) the young should "have access to the methods of the family planning of their choice."

At the same time as this conference was going on, the *Third World Forum of Youth* was held at Braga. Supported by the UN (29 representatives of UNFPA alone were registered at the Forum!) and especially by the UN Youth Unit and various nongovernmental organizations, this forum was to publish the *Braga Youth Action Plan.* Members of the anti-life and anti-family establishments encountered real opposition from the young. The president of the World Assembly of Muslim Youth, Altaf Husain, spoke prophetically when he declared: "Your attitude is fundamentally that of a liberal European minority, and you are on the way to imposing it."

4. *The Declaration of the Defenders of the Rights of Man* had first been discussed in Geneva and was supposed to be taken up in the summer session of the Economic Council. This declaration was aimed at protecting those "working for the rights of man." It had two objectives: to defend the "workers" propagating the "new rights of man" and pursuing those who are opposed to these same "new rights."[23] We know that among these "new rights" figure abortion, homosexuality, the polymorphous family, the nonresponsibility of parents for their children, etc.

Again in the summer of 1998, an accord was passed among UNFPA and the UN High Commission for the rights of man with a view to promoting "reproductive rights," the rights of women and population control.[24]

5. It was no surprise, then, when Nafis Sadik announced in her opening discourse the color of the annual conference of the nongovernmental organizations assembled by the UN in New York on September 17, 1998. The themes she insisted on needed to be hammered away at heavily in the course of the next months. One must expect that "reproductive freedom" on a worldwide scale be incorporated in one way or another in the "new rights of man." This "reproductive freedom" would have to include the "right" to abortion. As for adolescents, they should also be "liberated from all sexual restraint."

6. Not tiring of seeking new alliances, UNFPA signed an accord with the Islamic Conference, uniting 56 States. This accord aimed at facilitating cooperation between the two entities in the area of population control, reproductive health and the family.[25] In the end, it was to neutralize Islam, which often showed itself attached to life and the family, at the big international conferences organized by the UN.

7. On October 20 and 21, 1998, the UN Environment Program (UNEP) sponsored in New York a cycle of conferences on the theme "Ecology and Religion: To Discover Common Ground." It appeared that the concern of the UNEP, and other agencies and programs, as well as several nongovernmental organizations, was to create a new world religion. According to the vow of Gorbachev, the Earth Charter was supposed to replace the Decalogue. More intrepid still was the project presented by a certain Wangari Maathai (Kenya) to rewrite the Bible! Is that all!

In fact, the aim was to attack the monotheistic religions—Jewish, Christian, Islamic—in order to be able to relaunch the old pantheisms.[26]

The 1999 Programs

For the period of 1999, several important meetings should be taken into consideration.

• *The Hague*

The *Hague Conference* (Feb. 8-12, 1999) had been prepared by meetings held in Kampala (Uganda) and Dhaka (Bangladesh); it brought together 179 States, all members of the UN. As usual, it entailed international meetings that were not intergovernmental.

From Feb. 4th to the 6th, the International Forum of Members of Parliaments took place at The Hague, assembling 210 deputies from 103 countries.

Feb. 6th and 7th saw the Youth Forum, continuing that of Braga (1998), assemble some 120 young people. The habitual themes were treated. One had to acknowledge the right of youth to be assisted in the exercise of their reproductive rights. In plain language that meant that they should have access to contraception and abortion, without their parents having the right to interfere. According to the Forum, these reproductive rights of youth must be universally recognized.

In between the Youth Forum and the intergovernmental conference, the *Forum of Nongovernmental Organizations* was held. And we shouldn't be surprised to find the same recurrent themes taken up: the advancement of women via the promotion of reproductive health and rights, gender, etc. The great moment in this forum was the intervention of Hillary Clinton. In view of the Beijing+5 Conference, Mrs. Clinton pleaded that all women be given access to abortion and that this be recognized as a "human right." Foreseen by some as the successor to Nafis Sadik, the president's wife made an appeal for funds for the population control programs. UNFPA had received but 25% of the sums promised it at Cairo.

The objective of the *Intergovernmental Conference* at The Hague was the preparation of the ICPD+5, that is, the big conference that, after five years, was to render an account of the application of the Cairo Conference and trace a plan of action for the future: this big conference was to be held in New York from June 30th to July 2nd, 1999. The organizers of The Hague Conference hoped for a vigorous affirmation of the connection between, on the one hand, Cairo's plan of action, and on the other, certain documents, whether before or after the Cairo Conference.

Among the earlier documents figures the Convention for the Elimination of All Forms of Discrimination Against Women (CEDAW). This convention dates from 1979. The organizers of The Hague Conference were urging States to ratify this convention quickly. In so doing, national legislation would be led to protect the "rights of women," including abortion. In like manner, it would be necessary to exploit the final document of the Vienna Conference on the rights of man (1993).

A post-Cairo document, the platform of action established in Beijing (1995) would also have to be exploited. The Hague Conference could not, then, neglect insisting on *gender*, not only repeating the can-tilena of "reproductive rights," but also giving validity to homosexual claims. Supporting homosexuality, in effect, is part of the tactics that have to be used to control population growth. In brief, it is a question of invoking in all these cases intersecting references in order to give more weight to the "reproductive rights" that Cairo presented as an integral part of its program for population control.

As a corollary, The Hague Conference launched an appeal to fight against all the "negative, traditional, religious and cultural practices" opposed to "reproductive rights," that is—according to the organizers—to women, as well as to the "gender perspective," and notably homo-sexuality.[27]

Let us point out in this regard that, as in other circumstances, the organizers took care to invite Frances Kissling, the leader of the radical feminist movement "Catholics for Free Choice." Benefiting from obscure resources, this Trojan Horse (namely, the movement) fraudu-lently usurps the label "Catholic" to sow confusion. And the deception succeeds sometimes, for the rip-off merchants always find some unsus-pecting people all too willing to let themselves be duped.

Thus do the agencies of the UN confirm a practice that is usual among them. Passing itself off as source of "the new rights of man," and imposing them on nations, notably by means of international juridical instruments, the UN uses the *salami tactic*: it nibbles away at the sov-ereignty of nations and passes itself off more and more openly as a mechanism of world government.

The conference at The Hague ended without its achieving the draft-ing of a final document. Prepared by UNFPA, the latter could hardly restrain its surprise.

• *Toward a General Assembly*

Besides the Conference at The Hague, various other meetings took place in the course of the first semester of 1999. We remain confound-ed by the funds used for innumerable, incessant and exorbitantly costly meetings which continue mulling over the same themes like incanta-tions. And so we will limit ourselves to mentioning summarily a few meetings at which population control took a central role.[28]

The Commission on the Status of Women (CSW) met in New York from March 1st to the 19th. Two matters were successively taken up.

First, the Optional Protocol concerning CEDAW (the Convention for the Elimination of Discrimination Against Women), which was adopted on March 12. Let us point out that this Optional Protocol provided for legal proceedings in case of "serious or systematic violations of the rights of women." This commission also looked into the preparation of the fifth anniversary, in 2000, of the Beijing Conference, that is, Beijing+5.

The UN Commission on Population and Development (CPD) met in New York from March 24th to 31st.

From April 4th to the 17th a Round Table was held in New York on the rights and the sexual and reproductive health of adolescents.

The Commission on Sustainable Development (CSD) was held in New York from April 19th to the 30th.

The committee to prepare the fifth anniversary of the Copenhagen Conference in 2000, that is Copenhagen+5, met in New York on May 17-18.

• *The Special Session of the General Assembly*

Prepared, as we have seen, by a spellbinding whirlwind of meetings, the special session of the General Assembly, known by the initials ICPD+5 (International Conference on Population and Development), was held in New York from June 30th to July 2nd.[29]

It was directed by UNFPA. Skipping over the scientific conclusions of other agencies of the UN and, to top it off, ignoring the dossier she supported in 1998,[30] Nafis Sadik asserted right from the beginning that the world had to watch out for the "demographic bomb," especially in the Third World countries. In his inaugural address, Mr. Kofi Annan, Secretary General of the UN, himself imprudently opened the way by suggesting, not without audacity, "that the demographic growth of the planet had to be stabilized."

To face this so-called "bomb," Madam Sadik, supported by the nongovernmental satellites of the UNFPA, went on to advocate various measures. Here are the principal ones:

• One must continue to fight for abortion as a universal "sexual right," and access to it must be facilitated.

— In countries where the law is opposed to abortion, the governments will have to modify the legislation in this regard; in such cases, they will benefit from incentives or be subject to pressure.

— The calendar is fixed: by 2015 one and all will have access to the services of health and family planning, including abortion and sterilization.

— The conscience clause has finally been eliminated; nonetheless, it has been provided for health-care givers who do not wish to practice abortion.

— A program of sexual education for minors has also been provided in which "responsible behavior" is foreseen; finally, the rights of minors to abortion without consent of their parents will have to be promoted.

This ICPD+5 Assembly was surprising in more ways than one. It was supposed to *evaluate the application* of the plan of action elaborated at Cairo. However, at the ICPD+5 the Cairo conclusions were *discussed again and even modified*:[31]

— at Cairo it had been decided that abortion could not be considered as a method of birth control; five years later, abortion was presented, from the beginning of the Assembly, as the first measure to adopt toward this end;

— at Cairo there was certainly a question of population but also of development; at the ICPD+5, reference to development was in the main erased;

— finally and above all, the ICPD+5 outdid the roaming that had already tarnished the Cairo Conference: in 1994, the need for a plan to curb demographic growth was not considered necessary; now such a need was taken for granted and the ensuing plan necessary as well. On this essential point the organizers of ICPD+5 gave proof of an unexplainable offhandedness. In effect, if in 1994 the demographic decline was already recognized by the scientific community, in 1999 it was widely confirmed and admitted by the most honest international political authorities. Whence the question: what credibility can be given to international organizations that continue to wish to impose programs of action based on scientific falsehoods?

The Road for the Year 2000

The intergovernmental process leading to the special session of the General Assembly in 2000 is already en route. Several preparatory meetings are already organized.[32] The common goal of these meetings is to impose some "new rights" on the international community. All these conferences would have to subscribe to the "new rights of man" in their most radical formulations. It would be a question, understand well, of promoting abortion, homosexuality, etc. But these "new rights," and especially the "rights of women," would have to be imposed as international *juridical* norms. A universal code of conduct would, then, supplant the traditional norms, national legislations, cultures and, without doubt, religions.

[1] With regard to these questions which we are tackling, see the well-documented article of Seamus Gimes, "From Population Control to 'Reproductive Rights' Ideological Influences in Population Policy," *Third World Quarterly*, 19,3 (1998) 375-393.

[2] All the clichés of (neo)malthusianism and of demographic control appear in the *Dossier d'information sur la population et de développement* published in London by Marie Stopes International, 1994. For IPPS see p. 83.

[3] The sensitivity of the populations of African origin appears in the documented and vigorous work of Elizabeth Liagin, *Excessive Force: Power, Politics & Population Control* (Washington: Ed. Informations Project for Africa, 1995).

[4] See Paul and Anne Ehrlich, *Ecoscience: Population, Resources Environment* (New York: W. H. Freeman, 1977).

[5] See Zbigniew Brzezinski, *Between Two Ages. America's Role in the Technetronic Era* (Harmondsworth: Penguin Books, 19970).

[6] Robert McNamara, *A World Demographic Policy to Promote Human Development in the Twentieth Century* (New York: UN, 1991).

[7] This document is numbered NSSM-200/1974. Circulating in various presentations, this text can be found in the violently anti-Catholic work of Stephen D. Mumford, *The Life and Death of NSSM 200* (Center for Research on Population and Security, P.O. Box 13067, Research Triangle Park, NC 27790, 1994) 45-186. A summary and selected extracts were translated into French by Rene Bel and published by Trans-Vie 24 rue du Bourg, F-65100 Lourdes, France.

[8] One of the best overall works on demographic control is that of Betsy Hartmann, *Reproductive Rights and Wrongs. The Global Politics of Population Control* (Boston: South End Press, 1995; 1st edition 1987). See especially the chapter "The Population Establishment Today," 113-130. See also Stanley P. Johnson, *World Population and the United Nations* (Cambridge University Press, 1987). One may also refer to Milos Macura, "The Significance of the United Nations International Population Conferences," in *Population Bulletin of the United Nations*, 19/20 (New York, 1986) 14-25.

[9] According to this schema, admitted by the whole scientific community of demographers, in any given population one goes from high rates of births and deaths to low rates of births and deaths. Since the drop in mortality rate precedes the drop in the birth rate, one observes a natural growth of population during this transition. On this subject see our work *Pour comprendre les évolutions démographiques*, 39-41. For more details see Gérard-François Dumont, *Démographie* (Paris: Dunod, 1992) 113-115.

[10] Remember that in reality this growth continues to decline. And above all, a major change has occurred since 1992: the annual surplus of births over deaths has begun to diminish. (See on this subject our work *Pour comprendre les évolutions démographiques*, 21 f.) Demographic logic seems to be largely ignored by the leaders of these conferences, which confirms the ideological—and not scientific—character of their construction.

[11] Cf. The final document, Chapter VIII, 25. The interventions of the Holy See's delegation in the major international conferences of the UN on population, life and the family have been published in an impressive collection by Carl J. Marucci. Provided with a good index, this work is entitled *Serving the Human Family. The Holy See at the Major United Nations Conferences* (New York: The Path of Peace Foundation, 1997).

[12] On the occasion of the fifth anniversary of the Rio conference, the WHO published *Health and Environment in Sustainable Development. Five years after the Earth Summit* (Geneva: WHO, 1997); on the question of population see pp. 20-25.

[13] An uncompromising appraisal of the Cairo Conference was drawn up by a group of specialists. Michael Cook (ed.), *The New Imperialism. World Population and the Cairo Conference* (Crows Nest, Australia, Little Hills Press, 1994).

[14] We discuss the ideology of "gender" in *The Gospel Confronting World Disorder* (St. Louis, Central Bureau, 1999) 21-28.

[15] Following the Beijing Conference, President Clinton established the President's Interagency Council on Women. This council published *America's Commitment: Federal Programs Benefiting Women and New Initiatives as Follow-up to the UN Fourth World Conference on Women* (Washington, 1997). This publication makes it clear that the action of the US to advance the status of women constitutes "an important element of the external policy of the US." This element is inseparable from what is done in view of the North American interests in the areas of strategy, diplomacy and economy. (cf. The letters of Hillary Clinton and Madeleine Albright; see also p. 155).

[16] In order to evaluate the measure in which Cairo's program of action was applied, the UN's Division of Population prepared a detailed report entitled *World Population Monitoring 1996* and focused on *Selected Aspects of Reproductive Rights and Reproductive Health* (New York: United Nations, 1998). This report contains numerous tables concerning the demographic situation, but is concentrated on the "relatively new" and "controversial" notion of "reproductive rights."

[17] On this subject see Luc Ferry, *Le nouvel ordre écologique* (Paris: Livre de Poche, 13565, 1998), esp. pp.26-29, 194-199, etc.

[18] See the document of the Comision Economics para America Latina y el Caribe (CEPAL) entitled *Población, salud reproductiva y pobreza*, 27th period of sessions, Oranjestad, Aruba, May 11-16, 1998, mark LS/G.2015 (SE5.27/20) 98-2-188, dated April 15, 1998. This can be rounded out with the *Annual World Bank Conference on*

Development in Latin America and the Caribbean. 1996. Poverty and Inequality. Proceedings of a Conference held in Bogotá, Columbia, edited by Shaid Javed Burki, Sri-Ram Aiyer, Rudolf Hommes (Washington: The World Bank, 1998).

[19] The radical feminists fought without success for the Court to recognize cases of "enforced pregnancy." According to the interpretation given by the radical feminists, this expression would mean that "every pregnancy not accompanied with the right to an abortion, should be denounced as an enforced pregnancy." Every State would then be obliged to liberalize abortion and it would be forbidden for groups and individuals to oppose that, *under penalty of being brought before the International Penal Court* for attacking the "new rights of man." It is clear that if the radical feminists have lost this battle, they are determined to remount the battlement at the next opportunity with the help of homosexuals.

[20] See what we said earlier under *Rio, 1992.*

[21] On this subject see our works *The Totalitarian Trend of Liberalism*, esp. 81-87, and *The Gospel Confronting World Disorder*, esp. 112-120.

[22] Source: CAFHRI <www.cafhri.org> of Oct. 9, 1998.

[23] Chosen according to unexplained criteria, some extracts of this *Project de déclaration sur les défenseurs des droits de l'homme* were published in *Le Monde* (Paris) of Dec. 8, 1998, 19. This selection holds some surprises, like the total omission of art. 7, which is echoed in our text.

[24] Source: CAFHRI <www.cafhri.org> of Oct. 31, 1998.

[25] Source: CAFHRI <www.cafhri.org> of Oct. 16, 1998.

[26] Source: *Noticias de la ONU* <jcs@cvtci.com.ar> and CAFHRI <www.cafhri.org> of Oct. 3, 1998.

[27] A source providing *Noticias de la ONU* that cannot be overlooked is regularly published under this title by Juan Claudio Sanahuja at the address: <jcs@cvtci.com.ar>; see esp. the report of April 5, 1999.

[28] More details can be found about these activities at the UN's Internet site <http://www.un.org/>.

[29] The document adopted on July 1 is entitled *Key Actions for the Further Implementation of the Program of Action of the International Conference on Population and Development*; it bears the mark UN Document A/S-21/5. This text is available on the Internet at: <http://www.unfpa.org/icpd/reports&doc/chaiman-final.htm>. For more details concerning ICPD+5 see the following sites:

<http://www.pagina.de/noticiasdelaonu>;

<http://www.zenit.org/spanish/subenvivo.html>;

<http://www.aciprensa.com>;

<http://www.prolifeinfo.org>;

<http://www.c-fam.org>.

[30] See *L'Etat de la planète* 1998. The 1998 edition of this annual publication of UNFPA bears the title *Les générations nouvelles*. Prepared under the executive direction of Nafis Sadik, this dossier evokes the drop in fertility, the slowing of demographic growth, ageing. Cf. also the UN works mentioned in note 17 of Chapter I of this work.

[31] The Holy See's delegation did not fail to point this out. On the role played by this delegation at ICPD +5, see the dossier produced by Nathalie Duplan in *Famille chrétienne* (Paris) n. 1124 (July 29, 1999) 7-9. This article includes two interviews: the one of John Klink, a member of the delegation; the other of Tugdual Derville, director of the review *Ethique et Populations* (Paris).

[32] We will list the principal ones in Appendix IV.

CHAPTER V

THE UN AND AUTHORITARIAN POPULATION CONTROL

During the sixties, the time of military regimes, the "doctrine of national security" flourished in Latin America.[1] This doctrine had been forged in the rich countries, those at the "center," and exported to the countries on the "periphery." It maintained that the major problem was the opposition between the communist world and the liberal-capitalist world. The *dominant antagonism* was between East and West.

THE NORTH-SOUTH ANTAGONISM

Today, with an uncommon exuberance, the wealthy countries have reinterpreted this doctrine and see the actual dominant antagonism to be between the rich countries of the North and the poor countries of the South. Presently, the North is rich but represents only a fifth of the world's population. Thus the North imagines that the South constitutes a threat to its well-being, and this by reason of the demographic pressure supposedly coming from the South. Hence, just as the ideology of national security required "containing," that is blocking, the threat coming from the communist East, so must one today, according to the demographic ideology, "contain" the threatening demographic pressure coming from the poor South. In summary, it is a question of a radical reinterpretation of the idea of *total war*: the rich countries, older and with less population, must protect their supremacy at any price. The UN is the ideal instrument for this objective.

Actors and Victims

The protagonists of this confrontation are, first, the United States, especially through its Agency for International Development (USAID[2]), and secondly, Japan, Norway and the European Union, which, in this matter, has adopted an attitude objectively close to that of the US, aligned with world leaders.[3]

These countries, but especially the US, use mainly the UN and its agencies to increase and at the same time camouflage their interventions.[4] The chief agencies concerned are the World Bank,[5] the UN Program for Development (UNPD[6]), the UNCTAD (United Nations Conference for Trade and Development[7]), the UN Fund for Population Activities (UNFPA[8]), UNICEF, UNESCO, FAO (Organization for Agriculture), the WHO, etc.[9] The table which is subsequently shown is very explicit as to the involvement of the UN in this matter.[10]

The same rich countries consistently use certain nongovernmental organizations (NGO), such as the Population Council[11] (sponsored by the Rockefeller Foundation), the Ford Foundation, the MacArthur Foundation,[12] the Worldwatch Institute,[13] The Women's Environment and Development Organization (WEDO,[14] which had been dominated by the extravagant Bella Abzug) and some other organizations of variable weight. The most important is the IPPF.[15] This organization receives considerable sums of money, and it comes from governments, agencies of the UN, and private foundations. The exchanges of functionaries between the IPPF and certain governmental and international public organizations is very frequent: a typical case of cross participation!

As we have already indicated, the role of the nongovernmental organizations tends to grow, thereby justifying serious concern. In fact, while the public international organizations act more on the level of governments, the nongovernmental organizations, having enormous resources but lacking any representative mandate, have direct access to countries in which the population control programs have been applied. In many cases, UN agencies come to the point of delegating tasks to the nongovernmental organizations. These latter, then, perform tasks entrusted to them by virtue of an abusive subcontracting; they perform them while circumventing or neutralizing the control of national authorities.

It is not superfluous here to point out the European Union's position of principle such as it was defined immediately after the signing of the Maastrich Treaty (Feb. 7, 1992). In its program[16] documents, the Commission of European Communities also considers that "it is crucial that the demographic growth be brought under control" (p. 40). This demographic dimension of cooperation in development has been incorporated in the Convention of Lomé (art. 155) and in the Protocol with the South and East Mediterranean countries (MSE, cf. Art. 3). We find it again in other Community documents.[17]

Family planning is presented as a "fundamental social service" (p. 87). In a more general fashion, questions about population have acquired a priority and are considered as "one of the essential components of development policy" (p. 89). "This attention is fully justified by the fact that the demographic growth of numerous developing countries is excessive" (*ibid.*). The document nevertheless concedes that fertility has dropped and that "action in this area makes no sense in itself, but only as an element of the policies of social and economic development whose effectiveness is conditioned by it" (p. 89). It nonetheless remains true that "the solution to problems of population appears as an essential condition of enduring development" (*ibid.*). The arguments reprised by the Commission are well known: imbalance between the number of people and resources and/or wealth, environment, women's rights, existence of a demand for family planning, shift in behavior, responsibility of States, etc.[18]

The *victims* are the countries of what we call the Third World in general, and more precisely the poor segments of the population of these countries, often defined with a barely hidden racist connotation.

Those who *oppose* this are relatively few but are increasingly active. They are the delegates of the Holy See; nongovernmental organizations for life and/or for the family, of which many are Catholics; the Group of 77, which today represents some 113 developing countries, delegates from Muslim countries attached to life as a gift from God, etc.

Recurrent and Intertwined Themes

The essence of the propaganda on population disseminated by the UN and the wealthy countries includes three basic references: to Malthusianism, neo-Malthusianism, and living space. We have already presented these themes and observed that they are at work in successive conferences. Some derived themes have been grafted little by little onto the initial core and are brought out according to the opportunities offered by the various meetings. *Malthusianism* is completed by the doctrine on "food security" and the scarcity of natural resources; *neo-Malthusianism* is clarified by means of the theme of "gender" and "new rights"; *living space* reappears under the label "surrounding environment" and the cult of Mother Earth.

Under the subject called "new rights" appear the themes of "reproductive health" including abortion; "new models of the family" including homosexual "families" to which are granted the right to adopt; sex education for children who must be freed from all parental rights, etc.

The theme of *consensus* merits special attention: it proclaims the *total rejection of all reference to objective criteria of truth, morality and justice*.[19] The great preoccupation of the international meeting organizers is to reach consensual decisions. Toward this end, they have to hide the always-numerous reservations formulated by the delegations from countries of less importance. This procedure tends to establish a new right of custom, that based on what is done—even by a minority—or on what appears in the decisions called consensual. And just as the ideological engineering allows them to modify *attitudes* and *behavior*, one can also modify the *juridical* norms of countries participating in the meetings, beginning with the plans of action that are the object of consensus. In this way, one institutes surreptitiously a *supranational* authority at the same time as one weakens the *sovereignty of nations*. *Henceforth nations won't control the UN; the UN will control them.* Moribund, the principle of subsidiarity?

This weakening of sovereign States is accelerating as a consequence of the inadmissible increase, by the UN itself, of the non-governmental organizations' involvement.

As one can notice, all these themes are intertwined. It was not by accident that, during the FAO Conference (Rome, 1996), James Gustave Speth, in charge of the UNPD, declared: "The UN has forged an integrated plan." In this "integrated plan," for example, the UNFPA and the WHO cooperate. The UNFPA had put a lot into the preparation of the "Earth Charter" and of the "Universal Code of Conduct" which—together with other declarations—could control the Universal Declaration of Man's Rights (1948). For its part, the WHO had elaborated a "new paradigm of health," that is, a new medical ethic which makes health a commodity which is more important than any other, one which may or may not be purchased according to criteria of economic priority: another misfortune for the poor![20]

It is possible, however, that a grain of sand has infiltrated this "integrated plan" as a consequence of the opposition, at the Second Earth Summit, to the idea of an "enduring development." Contesting a single piece of the integrated plan could lead to opposition to the entirety of the plan, or advance even further to the calling into question of the "new rights of man," already begun at the Braga Forum.

A Few Traps

It would be tedious to produce a list of *tactics* used by organizations controlling population. We will mention the principal procedures that directly affect developing countries. A staggering multiplication of *meetings* that burden the budgets of States; a deluge of repetitious *documents* which are almost always unreadable; the hegemony of the *English language*; the fantastic *imbalance* between personnel and resources, a part of which is used by the rich and another part by the poor; privileged access of the "controlling" establishment to sources of *information*; discriminatory *selection* of nongovernmental organizations admitted to participation in the meetings according to the degree of their involvement in the programs for population control; innumerable traps of *vocabulary* to mask inadmissible content, euphemisms, paradoxes, semantic transfers, etc; *salami tactics* which consists in obtaining slice by slice, piece by piece, what the "pigeon" would never concede as a whole; *subordination of "aid"* to acceptance of population control programs; *blackmail* or explicit or cunning *threats*; *corruption* of the national leaders of victim nations; *suborning* of the medical-hospital personnel to execute definite programs, for example, campaigns of sterilization.

PROCLAIMING THE TRUTH

Human Capital and "Natural Resources"

There are numerous morally and scientifically unacceptable assertions that form part of the ideology of demographic control. The agencies of the UN—UNFPA, World Bank, UNPD, UNICEF, etc.—commit a fundamental error; they hold that there is an established correlation between demographic change and economic growth. Now that is a *hypothesis that has never been demonstrated.* Consequently, it is absurd to base population control policies on a supposition so void of scientific foundation.

Confronted with the proliferation of inadmissible allegations, we believe it appropriate to assert some truths full of hope but often hidden or ignored, not only by some leaders and scientists but also by the media.

Some examples, briefly: the principal cause of world population growth must not be looked for in some unrestrained birth rates.[21] The principal cause is found in the general *increase in life expectancy* at birth as at every age. In other words, men live longer and longer and *consequently* they are more numerous as they occupy the earth *at the same time.*

Let us add that life expectancy at birth is the best synthetic criterion of development. Increase in life expectancy, seen almost everywhere in the world, contradicts head-on all the merchants of panic.

ILLUSTRATION 22

Change in life expectancy at birth:
Some examples

Period	USA		Russia		Japan		India	
	M	**F**	**M**	**F**	**M**	**F**	**M**	**F**
1900-1910	45,6	48,3	30,9	33,0	42,4	43,7	22,6	23,7
1950-1955	66,2	72,0	62,5	70,5	62,1	65,9	39,4	38,0
1990-1995	72,5	79,3	61,7	73,6	76,4	82,5	60,4	60,5

Source: According to Alene Gelbard *et al., World Population Beyond Six Billion*, p. 9.

The second most important cause is the demographic thrust or potential. A population can, in effect, continue to grow, for a certain time period, while fertility is in decline. Let us suppose that women of child-bearing age are less fertile than their mothers. It can happen that, globally, they have more children nonetheless because they are more numerous and subject to lower mortality rates than their mothers.

The production of foodstuffs is such that they don't know what to do with the surplus: today the principal problem is inadequate distribution. Thirty years ago India had less than three hundred million inhabitants and experienced terrible famines. Today, thanks to the "*green revolution*" begun by Norman Borlaug,[22] that is, thanks to the decisive discoveries accompanied by good political and economic decisions, India sustains nine hundred million people and exports cereals.

The sustaining capacity of the earth varies, in space and time, according to the ability of man to humanize the environment.

Many scientific studies show that today *human capital* involves much more than *physical capital*. That is what Gary Becker[23] had already shown in 1964. It was confirmed, for example, by the detailed studies of Julian Simon (of the University of Maryland) and Jacqueline Kasun (of Humboldt State University). We can even affirm, in a somewhat paradoxical manner, that there *are no natural resources*: it is man who, with his intelligence and thanks to education, transforms ordinary things (like sand) into riches (like semi-conductors and electronic equipment). All serious studies are currently in agreement in affirming that the primary cause of poverty is the *inequality of access to knowledge* as well as the poor sharing of this same knowledge.[24] The countries that have developed most since the Second World War are not those that have received the most aid (e.g., Zaire, Ethiopia); they are those that have exploited human capital (e.g., Japan, Taiwan, Korea, etc.). And, as Gary Becker has demonstrated, it is first of all in the *family* that human capital is formed.[25]

In the areas already mentioned and in many others, people have an enormous power of *invention and intervention*. We have no way of determining the limits of this power, any more than we are able to assign limits to human creativity. There is no fatalism about poverty. Those who invoked a determinist relationship between population and development are too often inclined to want to eliminate poverty by eliminating the poor.

Organizing

The partisans of population control are wealthy, organized and disciplined; they coordinate their work; they share tasks. They have a real level of *professionalism*; they are counseled by technicians who are excellent at lobbying (pressure groups), at social communication, at manipulating assemblies and television audiences, etc.

The defenders of life have much to learn in this domain. Most of the time, they act with a lot of good will but rarely surpass the level of generous amateurism. To limit ourselves to the Christian milieu, it even happens that the defenders of life do not succeed in motivating their own troops well, which would give power to their impact. In this situation, there are three kinds of remedy.

Study the "controller" methods of action and, without yielding in the least to cynicism, *be inspired by these methods* in order to serve life and the family. Such will be the object of our last chapter.

Profit to the maximum from the *numerous organizations*, Christian or not, that fight for life, and actively cooperate with them. There are many nonconfessional organizations that defend life and the family; Christians don't have a monopoly on this twofold defense program. However, we find, above all, many Catholic organizations very active in these areas, both on the national and international levels; many of them have a high level of professionalism. All of these organizations deserve to be supported personally, morally, scientifically and financially. Fighting actively within these organizations must be considered as a priority in the context of the "new evangelization."

Where practically nothing exists, it is imperative that a working group be established as soon as possible so that it be sponsored and counseled by organizations already experienced. A precise task merits priority attention: systematic work among politicians, doctors, journalists and businessmen in order to sensitize them to the evils engendered by an ageing population that is becoming scarce.

Denouncing

An integral part of working for life consists in the unreserved unmasking of the *abuses of power* committed in the name of population control. This may seem to be a gigantic task, but it must not intimidate us. The ideology of demographic security suffers from an irremediable weakness: it rests on scientific falsehoods and even on gross lies. It is inspired by a total disdain for those who are the weakest.[26] Consequently, it is appropriate to make every effort to have the actions of the UN agencies and of the nongovernmental organizations rejected to the extent that these activities involve programs of population control. Conditional aid enslaves and must be publicly denounced.

It is even appropriate to use the weapon of boycott to arouse national leaders to refuse payment of the UN assessments and the payment of subsidies to certain nongovernmental organizations. The boycott weapon always functions very well, as the difficulties encountered by laboratories that produce and distribute the RU-486 pill confirm. Along the same lines, after a campaign of sensitizing the media, it is advisable to demand that the authorities establish national investigative committees to find out whence come the resources destined for the control of countries' populations and in which slush funds they wind up.

Analysis of the recent international conferences and of the ideology inspiring them reveals the *extreme seriousness* of the attacks to which the human being is exposed as a consequence of the activities of those very people who should defend him. Since "man is the image of God" and "the glory of God is the living man," this situation cannot leave Christians indifferent. With good reason the Holy Father is *mobilizing* the Christian community: it is urgent that it unite and apply its forces to reverse the *culture of death* so that the *culture of life* may be victorious.[27] The UN's programs in the area of human life reflect the aggressive materialism, and the spiritual and religious desert of the present world, especially the world of the rich. The ideology spread across a dense network of institutional channels is an ideology of *fear* and *egotism*: fear that the rich have of the poor; the egotism of the rich; fear of the rich that, in sharing what they have and know, they will lose some of their quality of life.

---

[1] We have analyzed this doctrine in *Destin du Brésil. La technocratie militaire et son idéologie* (Gembloux: Ed. Duculot, 1973).

[2] USAID itself publishes some reports concerning its activities. See, for example, *Agency Performance Report 1996* (Washington: US Agency for International Development, January 1997) esp. pp. 1, 29; 3, 1-34; 4,1; on p. 5, 4 we read: "Humanitarian assistance is in the national interest of the United States and is considered an investment for the future." Like all the documents of USAID, this one reflects extreme concern for "national security" which would be threatened on all fronts: population, environment, biodiversity, etc. USAID has, among other things, financed the English and French editions of the important *Guide for Those Responsible for Family Planning*, prepared by Management Sciences for Health and Pathfinder International (West Hartford, CT: Kumarian Press, 1994).

[3] In the matter of population, the European Union will impose, as a condition for admission, that candidate countries adhere to policy programs and juridical instruments to which the Union has already subscribed. It would be interesting to study closely the position of the European Union in this area.

4 Different agencies of the UN join together to co-sponsor some programs. See, for example, UNPD/UNFPA/WHO/World Bank/Special Program of Research, Development and Research Training in Human Reproduction (HRP), Reproductive Health Research: the New Directions. Report 1996-1997, 25th Anniversary issue, edited by J. Khanna and P. F. A. Van Look (Geneva: WHO, 1996). The priorities of this program, including chemical abortion, are exposed on p. 61; the definition of reproductive health appears on p. 84. See also the *Annual Technical Report 1997*, edited by P. F. A. Van Look, (Geneva: WHO, 1998)

5 Regarding the activities of the World Bank, see, among other things, *Health, Nutrition and Population*, the Human Development Network (Washington: The World Bank Group, 1997); World Bank, Annual Report 1997, esp. 14-23.

6 See, for example, the *Rapport mondial sur le développement humain* 1998, published by UNPD (Paris: Ed. Economica, 1998).

7 UNCTAD (Conference of the UN for Commerce and Development) published *The Least Developed Countries 1997 Report* (New York & Geneva: UN, 1997). On the "pressure of population" see 77 f.

8 On the different activities of UNFPA, see, among other things, *Reproductive Health. Directory for Training Courses* (New York: UNFPA, 1996/1997 edition); see, for example, 28, 37, 45, 175. The resources claimed by UNFPA for its population control programs and for reproductive health were the object of a volume entitled *Resource Requirements for Population and Reproductive Health Programs* (New York: UNFPA, 1996)

9 See WHO's Public Health and Environment in Sustainable Development Five Years after the Earth Summit (Geneva: WHO, 1997). Like other UN organs, the WHO is not unaware that the present demographic tendencies are low, but it continues, nevertheless, to present itself as the "medical arm" of demographic control. On this subject, see the *Rapport sur la santé dans le monde 1998. La vie au 21e siècle. Une perspective pour tous* (Geneva: WHO, 1998). On demographic tendencies, see pp. 95, 109-115, 127-131, 195; on family planning, see pp. 84-86, 105-109, 202-211 f. One should refer to the report copublished by UNPD, UNFPA, WHO and the World Bank under the title *Reproductive Health Research: The New Directions. Biennial Report 1996-1997* (Geneva: WHO, 1998).

10 See Illustration 23.

11 From the Population Council, see the *Annual Report 1997* (New York) esp. the foldout on p. 13 and pp. 14-31.

12 The objectives of the MacArthur Foundation are explained in a pre-publication draft entitled *Grantmaking Guidelines* (Chicago, 1997?); see esp. A. 13-15, 18; the obsession with security appears on p. 22.

13 Cf. Linda Starke (ed.), Lester R. Brown et al., *Vital Signs 1997. The Environmental Trends that Are Shaping Our Future* (New York: Norton Company, 1997). This publication really ought to concede that the world's population is in the process of getting older (cf. pp. 124 f.).

14 This organization publishes a review called *WEDO News & Views* in New York. Volume 11, n. 2 (June 1998) is mainly devoted to Bella Abzug (1920-1998).

[15] *Le Rapport annuel 1997-1998* of the IPPF contains a special dossier on youth (pp. 12-20) and leans toward the "sexual health of adolescents." Among the innumerable other publications of the IPPF let us mention Imogen Evans and Carlos Huezo (eds.) *Family Planning Handbook for Health Professionals. The Sexual and Reproductive Approach* (London: IPPF, 1997).

[16] In *Horizon 2000* see the appendix on *Les rapports de la Communauté avec les pays en développement dans la perspective de l'Union politique* (text of May 15, 1992) 21-80 of the collection entitled *Politique de coopération au développement à l'horizon 2000* (Brussels: Commission des Communautés Européennes, 1996); see p. 39 f. in particular.

[17] In the collection cited above, see the dossier *Planification familiale*, pp. 81-94, and especially the *Communication de la Commission au Conseil et au Parlement européen sur la démographie, la planification familiale et la coopération avec les pays en développement* (dated Nov. 4, 1992) 82-90.

[18] One will find more indications of the attitude of the European Union in Simon Stanley and Sara Hyde (eds.) *Handbook on European Union Support for Population and Reproductive Health Programs* (New York: UNFPA and London: Marie Stopes International, 1995). Produced by nongovernmental organizations, the *NGO Newsletter* is published at Hilversum and Wide at Brussels; this latter review published, in April 1997, a dossier entitled *The Future of EU-ACP Development Cooperation, A Gender Position*. One of the hidden aspects of this community policy was exposed in *Deadly Exports: The Story of European Community Exports of Banned or Withdrawn Drugs to the Third World* (Amsterdam: WEMOS/Pharma Projects, 1991).

[19] On the manner in which "consensus" is built, see Betsy Hartmann, *Reproductive Rights and Wrongs: The Global Policies of Population Control* (Boston: South End Press, 1995), Chapter VIII: "Building a 'consensus' for Cairo and beyond," pp. 131-155.

[20] It would be interesting to compare the resources which the WHO allocated to AIDS with those it allocated to malaria. According to this organization, in 1999 malaria was the cause of death to one out of four children in sub-Saharan Africa.

[21] For more details on the examples mentioned here, see our work, *Pour comprendre les évolutions démographiques* (Paris: University of Paris-Sorbonne, APRD, 1995).

[22] On the research and activity of Norman Borlaug, see Gregg Easterbrook, "Forgotten Benefactor of Humanity," *The Atlantic Monthly* (Jan. 1997) 75-82; Charles Mann, "Reseeding the Green Revolution," *Science*, no. 277 (Aug. 22, 1997) 1038-1043.

[23] Cf. Gary Becker, *Human Capital* (New York: Columbia University Press, 1964). Schematically, *physical capital* includes *financial capital*, that is, a sum of money producing interest, and *technical capital*, that is , the material means of production: factories, machines, equipment, etc. As for *human capital*, it constitutes by means of instruction, know-how, qualifications, health care to all of which a population has access; it is a long-term investment, since it lasts throughout life. The investment in human capital is a priority in the fight against poverty.

[24] On this subject, see John Kenneth Galbraith, *La République des satisfaits. La culture du contentement aux Etats-Unis* (Paris: du Seuil, 1993), as well as Alvin Toffler, *Les nouveaux pouvoirs* (Paris: Fayard, 1991).

[25] Cf. Gary Becker, *A Treatise on the Family* (Cambridge: Harvard University Press, 1993).

[26] *Etat de la population mondiale 1998*, published in New York by UNFPA, is forced to recognize the drop in fertility and the ageing of the world's population. But that did not prevent UNFPA from repeating its habitual clichés: there are too many Africans, Asians, Latin Americans, etc.

[27] On the subject, see the fine book by Juan Claudio Sanahuja, *El grand desafío. La Cultura de la Vida contra la Cultura de la Muerte* (Buenos Aires: Serviam, 1995).

CHAPTER VI

REMEDY FOR IMPLOSION: TENDERNESS

If the present drop in fertility is impossible to ignore, we cannot fail to be surprised by the maladapted and ridiculous measures habitually advocated to confront the situation created by this fact. One is even embarrassed to have to recall a truism: to remedy the drop in fertility and its consequences, we have to take appropriate measures to stimulate fertility while respecting the freedom of couples. Generally, action required for fertility is mentioned as though *it were on the same level as others* while it is really the key to the problem. It is inadmissible for the evidence to be hidden frequently or not given its due weight. We must, then, denounce everything in the social environment that has a negative impact on fertility. However, stimulating fertility is translated positively into attitudes which welcome life, respecting what is specifically feminine, valuing the child and protecting the family.

Confronted by the situation that we have analyzed in the previous chapters, several series of actions must be envisioned. We will analyze some of them.

1. It is important, first of all, to harbor no illusions. The worldwide anti-life machine is well-oiled. It can function without the myth of "demographic explosion." The North American policy in the matter—adopted by all the rich countries—is, until this day, fundamentally the one determined by Henry Kissinger in *Memorandum NSSM 200* of the National Security Council. This report, whose existence the vast majority of Americans is unaware of, is entitled *Implications of Worldwide Population Growth for US Security and Overseas Interests*. The thesis is explicitly apparent: controlling world population growth is essential to the security of the United States.[1] The report explains how the UN and its agencies, as well as the nongovernmental organizations (IPPF, Population Council, the Ford Foundation, etc.) must be mobilized to control the so-called world "demographic explosion." It is not necessary, then, to cite a plot: it suffices to denounce a plan of action which anyone can easily access.

In order not to make this study too heavy, we will not give any estimated indication of the finances allocated to population programs, or of the sources of this financial support.[2] On the other hand, we provide below an organizational chart coming from the UN itself and showing evidence of the involvement of most of its agencies in population programs. See **Illustration 23**.

One must acknowledge the fact that the UN agencies and numerous nongovernmental organizations had not waited for the Kissinger Report in order to intoxicate public opinion with their "demographic terrorism," nor to reap its attractive benefits. We must face facts: the drop in fertility is a gigantic business which profits the regiments of useless technocrats, corrupt governments, shady politicians, bought media, hospitals, laboratories, mercenary doctors, and a whole shabby cohort of charlatans of every kind who angle after the laughable bonuses dished out for their lowness.

In such a machine, *each one is hostage to the other*: we are in the presence of a web characterized by solidarity in corruption and by a law of environment which they hardly dare to break.

Illustration 23

The UN and Its Activities in the Area of Population

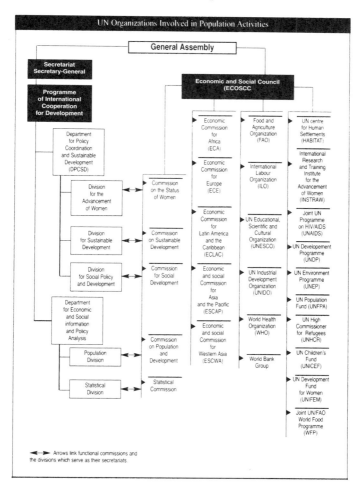

Source: Cynthia P. Green (ed.), *Profiles of UN Organizations*, Washington DC, Population Action International, 1996, p. 6.

Hence, if we have reason to rejoice over the initiative of the Population Division, we must nonetheless recall that one swallow does not make springtime. Nonconformist though it is, an initiative such as the meeting of experts (November 1997) should not make us forget that, in the *Titanic's* fashion, the decline in fertility is so *programmed and organized* in the world that one wonders how to ward off this announced disaster.

2. It is also appropriate to learn about the long-term programs of the UN in the matter of population and human rights. These programs are the object of incessant and extremely costly international conferences, sometimes well-covered by the media, sometimes narrowly escaping being clandestine, nevertheless having a constant: namely, the careful screening of agents and participants. These conferences offer a perfect illustration of the "salami tactic," which consists in obtaining slice by slice, conference after conference, what could never be obtained in block, which is what we sometimes call "whittling away."

Presently we are witnessing an evolution in the UN's strategy concerning population. This point has been emphasized recently by Dr. Marina Monacchi, of the Pontifical Council for the Family. The language of demographic fear is coupled today with talk about "new values." As we have mentioned in point 1 above, the anti-life programs have for their motive the fear of a "demographic explosion." Unfortunately for the ideologues of this myth, the evaluated data more and more clearly undermines the foundation of this fear. Despite their cynicism, these ideologues will not be able to repeat their oracles about the so-called "explosion" indefinitely, since demographers with integrity and other specialists have provided evidence, in an irrefutable scientific manner, of the drop in fertility rates and its consequences.

The ideologues of the neo-Malthusian myth must, then, be forced to revise their line of discourse. As Dr. Monacchi says so appropriately, "demographic control is no longer a 'remedy' to a 'problem,' but contraception, sterilization, homosexuality, etc. have become 'values' to promote." Whence comes a new trend, which, abusing the fiftieth anniversary of the Universal Declaration of Human Rights (1948-1998), extols the "new rights" obtained by way of "consensus" and endlessly renegotiable. These so-called "new rights" especially include "reproductive rights," corresponding to aforementioned "values."[3]

From that also flows the proclamation about the "polysemous" or "polymorphous" character of the family. This word can henceforth refer

90

to almost any kind of "consensual" union: heterosexual, homosexual, lesbian, monoparental, male or female, incest, each case able to be the object of a contract, voidable practically at any moment by one of the contracting parties. Curiously, bestial unions are hardly mentioned in the catalog of these "new rights." Forgotten? one may ask ironically. In any case, one can depend on the ecologists to protect animals against any form of coercion and to authentically interpret their enlightened consent!

3. The clarity which we have just shown is, however, not sufficient. We must urgently take certain measures. The first of them is summed up in a truism, for which we beg pardon of the reader, but which it is imperative to reaffirm. This truism is: since chemical contraception, abortion, and sterilization figure among the principal causes of the drop in fertility rates, we must use every means available to *curb these noxious practices* and reconsider the laws authorizing them.

4. One must also revise the model for State welfare. If one does not revise it calmly, it will have to be done in an emergency, but then it will be too late. In all the countries of the European Union, the taxation system is without credibility. The costs of production are much too high. All the world knows it; many are saying it. But the public authorities, so quick to inflate an inefficient bureaucratic clientele, show less imagination when it comes to protecting the ABC's of healthy economic relations: initiative, creativity and competition. Excessive taxes destroy employment, discourage the young, smother initiative, penalize the family, and encourage fraud, corruption and the black market. It is, then, fundamental to promote conditions that are favorable to the creation of new jobs. For example, numerous jobs, ensuring worthwhile services, could be created if the sponsor's costs—the tax on physical persons, surcharges, etc.—were not so high. The repercussions that would follow would undoubtedly favor fertility.

5. For the same reasons, it is urgent that the *unions*, taking more account of the common good, abandon their conservative demands and stop defending corporate interests which look very much like privileges. The profits resulting from the increase in productivity could create savings that generate jobs, as we have explained earlier. Moreover, the savings made available through increased productivity must not be monopolized either by the State or individuals: by the State, through a system of abusive taxation or a system of financing uncontrolled public deficits; by individuals, through demands coming from different categories of citizens. The escalation of corporate demands is contrary to solidarity, not only among workers, but also between generations. This escalation is a factor in marginalization and even in exclusion.

The system presently dominant has the amazing ability, not to generate jobs, but to produce excluded people at almost every stage of life. It makes many feel that they are not wanted. According to this suicidal logic, the lessening of fertility can easily be presented as a contribution to the solution of the problem of unemployment and exclusion.

6. One also notices all too infrequently that the increase in productivity masks the demographic deficit. One arrives then at proposing suicidal demographic measures, such as a reduction in work time and lowering the age of retirement. In a society where the proportion of dependent elderly persons does not stop growing by reason of the constant increase in life expectancy, to lower the age for transferring people to the category of dependent persons is totally unrealistic, all the more so as life expectancy without incapacitation increases. To this demographic consideration we must add that, even from the simple economic viewpoint, the investment in education must be amortized by a sufficient period of activity.

As J. K. Galbraith remarked, we live in the "republic of the satisfied," in the "civilization of contentment."[4] Having lost the notion of time, rich societies lose the sense of solidarity. Not content to reap the fruits of the labor of past generations, these societies live beyond their means. They go so far as to spend the revenues of future generations onto whom is transferred the payment of these debts. Captivated by consumerism, these societies live on deferred payment: they burn up today what future generations will have vital need of tomorrow. The drop in fertility has, in effect, this psychological drama: in the absence of descendants, numbers of people forget to envision the time beyond their own death: "After us, the deluge!"

7. In the final count, the best way of blocking the decline in fertility is to seek courageous family policies. Actually, these policies are not only, so to speak, nonexistent, but if some exist, they are trimmed under the pretext of budgetary economy or of dependent allowances!

We see everywhere the violent contrast between, on the one hand, the decline in fertility and the ageing of the population, and, on the other, the slowness of appropriate policy decisions. Some first-class specialists have nevertheless offered realistic proposals regarding this.[5]

Up to the present, the politicians have hardly paid any attention to their works. Just as merchants of contraceptives don't investigate the necessarily increasing decline in their market, politicians don't ask how many voters their party will still have in a generation.

8. Today, under the combined influence of communism and neoliberalism, women are not considered except insofar as they participate professionally in production. "Women in the home" is socially discredited and politically of little interest. The amount of time parents devote to the home is hardly acknowledged.

It is nevertheless urgent to reestablish the value of maternity. It is, first of all, a duty to acknowledge her who gave life to each of us. Public opinion must discover that maternity is not only a good for the mother herself, her husband, and her children, but also a good *for society*. It is, then, in the interest of society to create such conditions that those women who so desire may become mothers and take care of their children. The immense majority of young women interviewed regarding their future projects are in accord in saying that they wish to have several children. We must recognize the fact that society has multiplied the obstacles to the realization of this project. At the very least, women, in concert with their husbands, should be able to make this choice in a truly free manner: those who desire to be mothers should be able, without being blamed, to blossom in their maternity; those who choose to engage in a professional activity should be able to do so without fear; those who wish to reconcile being a professional and a mother should be able to fulfill this twofold level of their personality.

9. Finally, we cannot underestimate the decisive contribution which the Catholic community can bring to the world crisis in fertility. This contribution of the Church is first of all *doctrinal and moral*. Its foundation is based upon Christian anthropology, the theology of marriage, conjugal morality and social morality. The contribution of the Church is also not less important on the level of practical involvement.

Many Christian institutions are in a position to sensitize public opinion, the decision makers, the media, etc., about this crisis. One thinks of all the networks which the Church has at her disposal in the areas of education, formation of youth and adults, and communication. Also, the Church has founded and motivates thousands of charitable institutions and hospitals through which she can bear witness to the price she puts on life. Toward this end, a special and magnificent role falls to Catholic universities.

Catholics must also coordinate their public activity in favor of life and the family. Under the vigorous impetus of John Paul II and of the Pontifical Council for the Family, considerable progress has been made in this direction, thanks to the wide recourse to the Internet and e-mail, among other things. But the potential for development remains considerable. All the Christian family movements could be mobilized and their efforts coordinated to give couples the sense of joy in welcoming life.

Lastly and above all, Catholics must discern the call to *conversion* to which the facts direct them. The demographic decline experienced by Italy and Spain, "Catholic" countries if there ever were any, shows all Christians to what depths the rejection of *Humanae Vitae* leads.[6]

Toward a Culture of Life

If everything is not done to spread the culture of life, then the drop in fertility will fatally lead the human community to some dramatic problems. We can, alas, already at present foresee the extent and gravity of these problems.

The basic data to take into consideration can be summed up in a flash. If we keep to the data published by the *World Population Data Sheet 1999*, sixty-six countries of the world have a fertility index located below 2.1 children for each childbearing woman.[7] Let us remember that this level corresponds to the median number of children necessary to renew populations in the countries enjoying the best health conditions.

From the review we have just given, it follows that the major challenge facing humanity is twofold. It is a question not only of managing an ageing population but also a question of a decreasing population. The first need is already perceptible in most countries of the world; the second appears already in roughly twenty countries and in a number of regions. This twofold need is more or less obvious in various cases according to the different timetables of a given country. However, this tendency is becoming generalized very rapidly.

The causes of the foreseen *demographic implosion* are complex, but one cause is clearly the most important: the *growth of the population* is considered an evil that must be curbed as smallpox was curbed or as one tries to control malaria or AIDS. The erroneous character of this diagnosis has been scientifically demonstrated many times over. But this ideological premise is "necessary" to give deceitful legitimacy to antifertility programs in which most of the UN agencies are collaborating along with a considerable number of nongovernmental organizations and national governments.

To reverse this tendency, whose horizon is death, a diverse series of urgent measures must be taken.

The first consists very simply in *making known the factual truth*, placed at our disposition by demographers who have produced scientific data and refuse to become subservient to the sorcerer's apprentice, and whose predictions point the way to demographic implosion.

The second consists in *mobilizing the international community in order to purge the UN of a plethora of cynical technocrats* who live off the exploitation of sterility and death.

The third consists in sensitizing the same international community into *stopping the extensive financing, both public and private*, currently allocated to the fight against the transmission of life. A cessation of dues payments, as a form of resistance, is above all a question of survival for the States targeted by these programs.

The fourth consists, for the same States, in instituting *commissions of inquiry to examine the sources of these resources* allocated to the control of populations and to denounce those that are profiting from them. These inquiries must include calling for the examination of *external aid* often given on condition of accepting authoritarian programs of controlling fertility.

The fifth consists in reallocating budgets devoted to controlling fertility by applying them to intensive programs *to fight against death, to welcome life*, to help the family, to protect mothers, to feed the poor, to increase health care and education, etc.

The sixth consists in *giving rise to reforms aimed at more justice in society*. The most urgent of these reforms include sharing the knowledge, the *savoir-faire* and the resources we have.

Nevertheless, *these measures, and others, will remain inconsequential if they are not inspired by a strong love of all men*. Men simply must find once again the power to love more. During a television transmission made shortly before his death, Alfred Sauvy (1898-1990) shouted a cry of alarm regarding the fertility decline. And when someone asked him about the causes of this decline, the great demographer twice repeated with pounding words: "Today what most men lack is tenderness. . ."

---

[1] So that population control would be perceived and presented as a priority for the national security of the US, this is what appeared, among other things, in the bulletin published by the Alan Guttmacher Institute under the title *Washington Memo* (New York and Washington) 9-10 of December 1, 1997; it is also the theme set forth in a pamphlet intended for wide distribution, published in Washington, entitled *Why Population Matters,* published by Population International.

[2] One will find information on this subject in our works *The Totalitarian Trend of Liberalism* (St. Louis; Central Bureau, 1997) 30 ff; and *The Gospel Confronting World Disorder* (*ibid.* 1999) 9 f.

[3] This evolution has been studied in detail by Seamus Grimes in "From Population Control to 'Reproductive Rights'; Ideological Influences in Population Policy," *Third World Quarterly*, 19, 3 (1998) 375-393.

[4] John Kenneth Galbraith, *La Republique des satisfaits. La culture du contentement aux Etats-Unis* (Paris: Seuil, 1993).

[5] See, for example, Gerard-François Dumont, *Pour la liberté familiale* (Paris: PUF, 1986).

[6] As is known, the encyclical *Humanae Vitae* of Pope Paul VI is concerned with birth control; it is dated August 23, 1968.

[7] This document is published every year by the Population Reference Bureau in Washington. The Data Sheet of 1997 points out 59 countries.

CHAPTER VII

A LOBBY FOR THE POOR

Until now we have seen that the promotion of the family is the best way to counteract the drop in fertility. To conclude, we must return to a question that cannot be ignored: *What can we do*? It is a pertinent question, if there ever was one, for confronted by such determined and powerful organizations as those we have encountered, we often feel at a loss. One doesn't know where to begin. That is the reason why many are discouraged in advance and do not want to see the gravity of the situation or even to become informed.

In reality, there is much to do on different levels, even with reduced means. There is something to be done with every talent and purse. For instance, one can do some lobbying and exert effective pressure by the simple use and price of a postage stamp.

To facilitate matters, we will designate two levels on which action can be envisioned. These two levels correspond to Chapters VII and VIII. On the one hand is the level which we may call *informal*. Here private persons or a slightly structured group of individuals having similar sympathies can intervene. Whence the theme of this chapter: What kind of pressure can I exert? On the other hand, promoting life, the family and those human rights relating to them can be the object of much more systematic, structured and *professional* action. In this chapter we will examine what can be done by individuals. Our final chapter will be reserved for an inquiry into what can be done on a more professional level. One will notice, however, *that these two chapters will complement one another.*

1. The first thing necessary on the individual level is to become *informed.* And in those matters we have treated, the printed sources of information, always indispensable, have become distinctly insufficient. Traditional printed documentation circulates far too slowly. We need, then, to gain access to available information in real time and use electronic resources toward this end, in particular via the *Internet* and *e-mail.* By way of whetting appetites, in Appendix III we provide some Internet site addresses that merit a visit. As one will see, these electronic channels open a direct access either to agencies fighting for demographic control and the related practices or to some bulletins of information and commentaries emanating from pro-life and/or pro-family movements.

Let us state in this regard that a knowledge of *English* and even of *Spanish* is an unavoidable key for those who wish to have access to this information and to penetrate this medium.

Since the relation between knowledge and power is becoming progressively closer, it is also necessary to face certain facts: *Ignorance undermines power to the point of rendering it impossible to exercise it.*

2. Why not write to our particular government representatives to explain to them in a precise but brief manner what is taking place? These government officials are often swamped: sometimes they neglect to remain updated or simply don't have the possibility of doing so. The simplest thing, then, is to write and inform them, for example, about the coalitions organized and planned by the UN and its agencies. Have they heard about the "Declaration of the Defender of the Rights of Man" (*sic*!)? Do they know that at The Hague, in February 1999, there took place an important meeting to prepare for the ICPD+5? And what exactly Beijing+5 is? Are they aware of the stakes? Do they know the delegates who represent their nations during these meetings? The special duty of keeping informed is quite essential for European deputies. These, in effect, have the responsibility of formulating the positions defended by the European Union. How will the delegates be chosen? What control will the European Parliament and the national Parliaments be able to exercise over them?

Moreover, we need to sensitize national parliaments to the disastrous effects on the family of the legal policies accepted and provided for by "pacts of social union." Furthermore, it should not be difficult to remind parliamentary deputies, who are almost always parents, that they cannot either relinquish their responsibilities toward children, especially adolescents, or allow their supervision to be taken away.

Those are only a few examples. In practical terms, we should realize that a letter of more than one page has hardly any chance of being read. The best letter is one that does not go beyond making one point. Different points can be touched upon by messages coming from different correspondents. The essential thing is to *get their attention* and be ready, with further information, to satisfy their awakened curiosity.

An always effective initiative is to publicize the votes cast by each government representative during debates on life and the family. Voters have the right to know which officials voted for the proper promotion of family values and those who voted for abortion or sterilization. In Brazil, lists of names mentioning votes pro or con, as well as abstentions, are posted in public places, for example in some churches. Examination of these lists is always instructive, and voters will take these into account at the next elections.

While we are at it, one can envision the establishment of a permanent monitor by region or province. This monitor would be charged with publicizing how each elected official votes (or abstains) in matters concerning life or the family. With a little systematic work, it would be easy to set up a "rogues' gallery" of government deputies or candidates. The use of such a guide could provide voters with the criteria on matters which they hold most dear: respect for life and the family. This guide for voters would naturally be above party affiliations.

4. Voters would also take into account the clear, evasive or nonexistent replies received from candidates for election. Long before elections, any citizen is entitled to *demand in writing* from such and such a candidate what position he will defend when, for example, parental statutes or tax reduction for large families are at stake. At the same time, other voters could pose other questions on related matters.

5. Political parties are almost always constructed in a rigid manner, with a strong hierarchy abusing its power and a discipline in voting that compromises officials' representative character.

However, even in these parties, we meet free and independent spirits, disposed more to defend higher values than to look to their personal interests. *Such politicians deserve to be encouraged and supported.* Their action in favor of life and the family must be brought to the attention of the voters, especially large families and family associations. The party leadership cannot remain indifferent before the preference shown to such politicians and will be forced to take it into account.

6. Pro-life and pro-family circles constitute a particularly rich mine from which a new generation of politicians can arise. Until now, this mine has remained underexploited. The thing to do, then, is to stir up such vocations and to prepare the young for these roles.

7. In practically all countries, especially poor ones, TV spreads the Malthusian ideology. Often in the Third World, it provided commercials for sterilization. Starting with the case of Brazil, it has been established that TV was a powerful factor in the destruction of the family, and as a consequence, TV contributed significantly to the decline in fertility rates.

Anyone can write to the directors of TV stations to protest such harmful programs. It can be even more effective to pinpoint the big advertisers that sponsor the TV programs. Why not invite these businessmen to cut the fees paid to these stations which, in both the mean and long terms, are raising obstacles to the expansion of their firms by drying up the sources of potential clientele?

As in the domain of political action, this type of activity will be still more effective if a group were organized to watch *anti-life programs* appearing on TV. It will then be easy, every time the opportunity presents itself, to organize a massive campaign of letter-writing in protest, accompanied by a threat of *boycott*, to the firms that sponsor such programs.

8. The lack of information concerning attacks on life and the family is due to several factors. One of them is that newspapers and magazines depend on press agencies for the "news" they receive. One of the roles of these agencies, for that matter, is to hide or slant a good deal of the information they provide. Certain pressures are thus quasi-irresistible.

However, the best periodicals always want to inform their readers as completely and objectively as possible. To do that, they can count on specialized journalists and outside assistance. *A simple letter to the editor can trigger the desire to print a report*, to undertake an inquiry comprising many aspects of our discussion. In the matters we are considering, what are the UN, the UNFPA, the IPPF, the European Union doing? Where are their considerable financial resources coming from? An outline for such letters is available with the material in Appendix II. Not long ago, *LePoint* had a scoop by denouncing the bureaucratic waste of the WHO. There is a fine breeding ground to exploit.[1]

9. The instruction given to children in schools is also a domain which holds many surprises. By questioning their children or simply by talking with them, parents will often be astonished to learn what is being taught to their children—and what is being taught under the guise of sex education, biology, geography and even courses in religion. Mentioning geography may seem incongruous at first glance. But it is often within the framework of geography that they peddle the neo-Malthusian gossip about limits to population growth, lack of food, overpopulation, etc.

Participating in parent-student associations and dialoguing with the professors and directors of various establishments can offer an opportunity to clarify matters. It is also an occasion to recommend selected and adapted audiovisuals.

From this it follows that interventions before school authorities must be completed by *approaching the publishers of school books*. In the case of manuals on sex education, one must closely examine whatever treats the so-called "new rights of man," "reproductive health," the ideology of "gender," etc. In the matter of geography books, it will be necessary to remove whatever treats the Gaia cult and the ideology of demographic control. Manuals of biology must also be the object of special vigilance, since human biology borders on anthropology and, hence, involves a reflection on values.

10. Numerous are the pharmaceutical firms which earn large profits from the fight against life. The products they fabricate are regularly mentioned in the publications of UNFPA or the WHO. Such is the case of Norplant, Depo Provera, and RU-486, to cite only a few of the best known.

In this regard two kinds of action can easily be realized. The first is *informing others*. The undesirable effects of hormonal contraceptives are regularly minimized or passed over in silence. They are, however, explained in several medical publications.[2] Likewise hidden is the abortive effect provoked, under certain circumstances, by some of the present hormonal contraceptives.[3]

Nevertheless, the most effective strategy in the pharmaceutical domain is to organize boycotts of the products fabricated by those firms which prepare drugs inducing sterility or death. This is precisely what Dr. Baulieu himself explains regarding the abortifacient pill RU-486, thereby setting the record straight with the Hoechst Company.

Here is what Dr. Aulieu declared in 1991:

It is precisely the directors of the American affiliate of Hoechst who have infected the opinion of the German headquarters. Hilger, its president, even if he is a Bavarian Catholic, has never been against the pill [RU-486]. But today he is afraid. And his fears are fed by certain old phantoms from the past. The Hoechst company was born after the war from the dismantlement of the I. G. Farben corporation, the industrial giant which, among other things, produced the gas for the Nazi extermination camps. Hilger is terrified by the idea that antiabortion groups will unleash a campaign about his continuing to kill as in Hitler's time.[4]

To boycott the products of these firms presupposes a minimum of sensitivity on the part of the medical and pharmaceutical corporations. But the range of pharmaceutical preparations today is so large that doctors have no difficulty in prescribing one product rather than another.

11. You can also *contribute your financial help*. For the activities described here, the financial resources needed are not all that great, as we have seen. However, since these activities should normally be expected to develop, one must provide for more resources. In general, people want to know to what and to whom they are donating, and we can readily understand this. Action in favor of life, poor populations and the family inevitably takes various and unforeseen forms. As an activity grows in size, as it is taken in hand by a group that wants to organize and intends to make it go faster, the question of resources comes up. Telephone costs, copying, translation, distribution, transportation expenses, etc. arise. One has to pay for conferences and eventually rent space. All that presupposes the sensitizing of donors of different capabilities as well as collection efforts.

12. Defenders of life have possibilities and talents that are quite diverse. The greater part of these talents can be put at the service of life. Let us consider a few examples. Let us say that for your profession you have equipped office space. Nothing prevents your placing "an ideal fraction" of this space and equipment at the service of life and the family. Also, if you are a seasoned Internet user, you can join with other web surfers to set up a site in order to spread information about life. All the sites mentioned in the second part of Appendix III function at moderate costs; their audience is nonetheless considerable. If you are a computer "junkie," you can offer your services to prepare the text, the layout, the updating of files, the classification of documentation, the financial management, etc. If you are a lawyer, doctor, nurse, mother of a family, a professor, etc., prepare yourself to debate in public: you may even wind up liking it.

13. For the benefit of various categories of people whom we have mentioned and of the widest possible public, it is easy to organize formation sessions. These can take the form of a conference for the public at large followed by a discussion, or a seminar, intended for such and such a category of specialists (teachers, catechists, doctors, lawyers, etc.). Naturally, this type of activity requires greater financial resources than a postage stamp. But on the one hand, pro-life speakers ordinarily do not expect to receive stupendous fees; on the other hand, if one provides quality information, the public finds it more natural to share the expenses.

This type of formation-information activity calls for reinforcement and follow-up. *Reinforcement* and deepening will be done by way of carefully chosen *books and other printed matter*. To insure a follow-up, one needs to collect, insofar as possible, the names and addresses of those who participated in the initial formation session. After that one needs to nourish their formation and reflection by putting brief articles or some *more elaborate documents* at their disposal.

This can be the beginning of a united and motivated group whose activity will perhaps take on greater breadth than that of individuals. We are going to examine this other type of activity in the final chapter.

---

[1] Cf. Sophie Coignard and Anne Jeanblanc, "Organization mondiale de la santé. Scandales et gabegies," *Le Point* (Paris) n. 1334 (April 11, 1998) 82-89.

[2] One can always refer with profit to the substantial article of Dr. Rudolf Ehmann, "Problems in Family Planning," *Anthropotes* (Rome) n. 1 (1991) 95-126.

[3] On this subject see Maria Luisa di Pietro and Roberta Minacori, "Sull'abortività della pillola estroprogestinica e di altri 'contraccetivi'," *Medicina e Morale* (Rome) n. 5 (1996) 863-900. See also our work, *Bioethics and Population* (St. Louis: Central Bureau, 1996) question 122.

[4] Text taken from the article of Carlo Gallucci, "La pillola maledetta," *L'Espressa,* Rome, (Oct. 20, 1991) 156-165; our quotation comes from p. 161. See also our work *Bioethics and Population*, question 76 f.

CHAPTER VIII

A PRO-LIFE ACTION PLAN

Our last chapter has a limited and precise objective: *to determine a plan of action for the defense of life threatened by programs of population control in countries of the South.*

For that purpose we are going to propose a *strategy* which we will define here as a systematic set of coordinated actions for the attainment of a determined objective. The *objective* to achieve consists *in convincing national leaders to adopt a strongly anti-Malthusian attitude of resistance to "contraceptive imperialism."*

The first version of this text was prepared for a meeting of Latin American politicians held at Rio in 1992. It owes a great deal to the suggestion of Michael Schwarz, one of the best specialists in the matter.[1] The present text also owes much to a brochure by Elaine Murphy.[2] She applied herself to producing a strategy in favor of population control. Nevertheless, she failed to notice that her proposed strategy can be perfectly used to oppose population control campaigns. We must, then, thank Elaine Murphy for having elaborated an *ambivalent* and reversible strategy, since it can be turned against itself. An easy task for us, one that brings to light the twofold merit of the person who suggested it.

Proposing a plan of action means that we must consider successively many points which, for the sake of clarity, will be numbered.

THOSE WHO UNDERTAKE THIS ACTION

It is the promoters who are going to launch and effectuate a pro-life strategy. Prepared for them, the plan of action presented in this chapter has the specific features of being of very *supple* and *adaptable*.

1. The promoters can be individual persons, associations or organized movements that are especially pro-life and pro-family and are not content with improvisation and empiricism. These promoters, on the contrary, want to articulate systematic and effective action. Besides, that is precisely what promoters of population control do.

2. In this plan we trace directives that could inspire *lobbyists, pressure groups*, consultants, and people engaged in *public relations*: all are specialists in persuasion. In this regard one will note how urgent it is to *professionalize* pro-life activity by getting this type of specialist involved.

3. This plan can be applied on *different levels*, local, national and international. It matters little on which level one starts.

4. The plan also has the advantage of being able to be launched and realized with *limited financial resources*.

THE GOAL

1. It is, above all, a question of stirring up a *strong desire to stop population control programs* among leaders.

This attitude must involve the rejection of the programs for population control, whether they emanate from the UN and its agencies (like the UNFPA, the World Bank, the WHO, etc), or the government of the US (for, example, through USAID), the European Union, regional organizations (like the OEA), national governments, nongovernmental organizations (like IPPF or the Population Council), etc., or elsewhere.

2. If, after an evaluation, one sees that this goal cannot be attained, one can go back to a less ambitious goal. This would be to convince various leaders to decide not to participate or cooperate in projects of demographic control.

THE TARGET AUDIENCE

The public to be addressed or targeted depends on the pre-determined goal.

1. To identify this public, it helps to reply to the following questions:

> *a)* Who can act in such and such a domain in order to achieve the objective?
> *b)* Who would be opposed to the realization of the goal?
> *c)* Who hesitates to support the objective?

2. The targeted public is always comprised of people who have *power* and who are *implicated* in the proposed action, or concerned about it.

These people have, *for example*, the power to influence public opinion (TV commentators, journalists, educators, militant feminists, specialists in publicity, etc.), to legislate, to determine or execute a policy or to finance a plan of action. They can also have scientific, cultural or artistic prestige, be involved in sports, or have moral, religious power.

THE MESSAGE

What Message?

a) A message addressed to this diverse public must lead to action.

b) The message should be formulated by taking into account some of the *specific interests* of each public group one wishes to reach.

c) In any case, in all its formulations, the message will have to be focused on the *central goal* of the action plan.

Testing the Messages

a) Before spreading them on a grand scale, the different formulations of the message will have to be *tested* on a sample of the specific public group to which the message is aimed. Once the sample has been evaluated, one will proceed to making the corrections, adjustments and alterations called for by the message.

b) Regarding the public at large, the message can include but *one sole positive idea*, well adapted and strong.

Summary Examples of Messages

Adapted to Particular Public Audiences

a) To National Legislators

Ageing weighs heavily on the whole nation. Without a young and dynamic population, one cannot defend national sovereignty, nor ensure pensions, nor enable insurance companies to operate.

b) To National Citizens who have the Power to Determine the Broad Lines of Political Life

One cannot tolerate foreign interference in the determination of national policy. Neither can citizens deliver their countries into the hands of foreign powers. Children are an investment, that is, an expense agreed upon today that will pay off tomorrow.

c) To a Nation's Citizens Who Execute Policies

For example to doctors: mothers and their children stimulate medical activities as well as pharmaceutical, hospital and scientific ones, etc.

d) To Businesspeople

Births stimulate consumption, production, expansion, the creation of markets and jobs. We do not know of one civilization that developed as long as its birth rate was low.

e) To Those Responsible for Communications

Their role and responsibility is to speak the truth, to seek justice and to seek the interests of their nation. It is their duty to inform people about what is going on in their country regarding population control; to publish the names of those who collaborate in such programs and vote for them; to reveal the sources of financial backing. They should incite reporting and inquiries into programs of demographic control, sterilization, etc. It is their responsibility to show the value of the family, the mother, to support agrarian, fiscal, health and educational policies that are more just.

f) To Feminists

It is theirs to respect the specifically feminine, to denounce the new forms of *machismo*, of alienation, of oppression, of manipulation.

g) To Intellectuals

They should be the voice of those who have no voice, protect the poor against ideological manipulation of which they are the victims and which often comes from foreigners.

h) To Lawyers

They must defend the rights of the poor and the weakest in society as well as physical integrity, personal autonomy, life, a State of law, the fundamental rights of man, and not give in to juridical positivism.

i) To Educators

Today the principal wealth of a country is its human capital. Educators should invest, not only in people's productivity (improve their output), but above all their ability (stimulate their creativity), promoting a good education on all levels, and making it accessible to all, including women.

j) To Religious Leaders

Preach the centrality of love of neighbor in the Gospel. Arouse people's responsibility for the defense of the weakest in society and for the respect of man as having been made the image of God.

BEARERS OF THE MESSAGE

Destined for different sectors of the public, the message, in its different forms, proceeds from varied sources. These sources are the persons or organizations which are going to carry the message to the targeted publics.

We distinguish bearers of two types.

Change Agents

Generally change agents do not form part of the targeted public, but they enjoy respect and credibility before the public. For example, they are: renowned international experts as well as national personalities enjoying irrefutable moral or intellectual credibility, or other celebrities; TV stars, artists, and sports personalities whom it is advisable to locate in each country. Such change agents have the capacity to influence people.

Public Opinion Leaders

In every group a personality stands out who exercises natural leadership. It is a good idea to discover who exercises such leadership in the targeted group. One should be aware that these leaders will have to be, by preference, good speakers. Public opinion makers are, for example:

— *doctors* who stand out in their medical group;
— *businessmen* respected by their group;
— *lawyers* whose authority is acknowledged by the world of jurists.

CHANNELS OF COMMUNICATION

These channels are the pathways that provide the *spreading of a message*, going from one person or group to another. They are of two types.

Means of Mass Communication

By means of this channel a few people enter into communication with many people. For example, there are TV, radio, newspapers, and letters sent in bulk mail.

109

This channel is *ideal for the public at large*. It is also ideal for those who have the responsibility of making decisions and who are sensitive to the media.

Interpersonal Exchanges

By means of this type of channel, communication is established with carefully *selected* people. For certain types within the targeted public, this channel is often the most effective.

a) It is concerned, for example, with top executives to whom one can pay a personal visit, or for whom one can organize meetings with small groups, for example, seminars. One can also plan *national* conferences; invitations to such a national conference are then restricted to members of this group. A national conference can in turn be followed by *regional conferences*.

b) These top executives have very little time. That is why one should leave them with a *personalized brief note*, a kind of briefing, as well as a pamphlet, brochure or article of documentation. Similar documents can be consulted and will permit them to go more deeply into any given point.

c) For *mid-level managers* one can employ the same type of channels but under an adapted form. For them, letters deserve special attention. One should not lost sight of the fact that a good part of tomorrow's top executives come from this intermediate category.

THE FORM OF THE MESSAGE

1. The form of the message is, of course, its manner of presentation. The number of possible presentations is infinite, since such presentations depend on the creative imagination of those who try to communicate as well as the diverse sectors of the public. Some examples of presentation are: *viva voce* (conferences, lectures, debates, panel discussions, etc.), brochures, prospectuses, press communiqués, leaflets, descriptive cards, briefings, pamphlets, graphics, posters, memoranda, summary statements, transparencies, photos with commentaries, sketches, theatrical plays, parades, congresses, audio or video cassettes, audiovisual films, etc.

2. The ideal form *combines* three things:
a) a *viva voce* presentation;
b) a *visual* aid (transparencies, graphics, posters, etc.);

c) a *written documentation* (leaflets, cards, brochures, a press communiqué, etc.).

3. The *qualities* of the form are:

a) *clarity* and *simplicity*, of the graphics for example;

b) *beauty*, the attractive character of the presentation;

c) *brevity*: summaries, conclusions with recommendations; use of different type fonts, big letters, italics, colors, etc. For the most important points, particular care with the graphic captions;

d) *exactness* and *updated quality* of data;

e) *timeliness*: showing the link between the information and the present preoccupations of society.

4. In any case, this form must take into account the three elements already mentioned:

a) the *source* or *bearer* from whom the message is coming;

b) the *public* to which the message is addressed;

c) the *channel* through which the message passes.

5. As a general rule, *the greater* the quantity of mail the recipient has to deal with, the less time he has to devote to a particular question.

If a top executive (politician, businessman, doctor, communications specialist, etc.) writes to another top executive, the preferred form of the message will be a *personal memorandum*. That means a synthetic document of *one* page, rounded off by means of a summary that facilitates a deeper study of a particular point.

THE TRANSITION TO ACTION

Once the prior steps have been carefully seen to, it is proper to determine a *plan* of action. This plan should include the following:

1. A *calendar*, with an indication of the time limits for the realization of the different steps;

2. A *test* of the message having the purpose of seeing whether, for example, the various prospectuses, pamphlets, posters, graphics or films will pass or not;

3. A plan of *distribution* which will determine:

a) to whom the message will be communicated;

b) by whom;

c) through which channel;

d) in what form.

EVALUATION OF THE COMMUNICATION

The evaluation is not limited to verifying whether the diverse steps have been well executed; it has above all the objective of knowing whether the activities have been effective. This evaluation concerns above all three points: the process or execution, the results and the impact.

Evaluation of the Execution

This evaluation has two aspects:

a) The quantitative review of the work

—From the quantitative viewpoint, what judgment should be made on the volume of work: number of meetings, prospectuses, cassettes, etc.??

—Where has the work been done: in the nation's capital, in what State, in which cities?

—Was the determined time frame respected?

b) The qualitative review of the work

Here one examines *how* the information was given.

—Was the targeted public reached? By whom?

—Through which types of channels?

—Have the messages been communicated by sources or bearers enjoying the best credibility and the greatest influence on the targeted public?

—Have the best channels been used to reach such and such a precise category of the targeted public?

—Was the form used suitable to the category of the targeted public?

—Were preliminary tests done?

—Was the time of the message's delivery opportune?

—Was attention diverted toward another interest, for example, did elections or a soccer championship game coincide with the time of the message's delivery?

Evaluation of Results

This evaluation raises the following questions:

a) Were the activities *effective*? Did they induce the desired *changes* that will permit the message to attain its objectives?

b) In addition, this evaluation of the results depends on two factors:

—It depends fundamentally on the exact knowledge of the original *objective*. As it happens, the objective is clear: to support a policy of rejecting programs of population control.

—It also depends on the *gauges of success*. These gauges can be, for example: a project of passing a law to improve birth conditions; legal measures for helping parents; fiscal measures ensuring better justice for the family; facilities for large families that need housing; access to all the levels of the educational system for the children of poor families; a wide public discussion of the present demographic policy; the publication of internal and external resources allocated to these policies; the distribution of the list of government officials who voted for or against programs of birth control; the proposing of a new population policy; a wide discussion and/or a new fiscal and/or agrarian policy in order to make new population policy possible, etc.

Evaluation of the Impact

The impact shows the stimulating power of the activities. Have subsidies for giving birth been decided? Have family allocations been created or improved? Has a statute to protect mothers seen the light of day? What has happened regarding family housing and aid for education? Has a fiscal reform taken place to make possible or to facilitate a family policy? Has there been an in-depth discussion about population policy?

Summary

1. Begin with the *promoters* of the plan.

2. *Formulate exactly the objectives* of the activity which is being planned.

3. *Identify the targeted public*, that is, the public one wants to motivate in order to attain the objective. Through the positions they express and the decisions they make, the members of this public have the ability of launching programs of action.

4. *Determine the content of the messages* that have to correspond to the preoccupations of diverse categories of the targeted public. One doesn't speak to a politician the same way as to a businessman or doctor.

113

5. *Identify the sources*, that is, the people and/or organizations who will be able to be bearers of the message to the targeted public.

6. *Choose the appropriate channels*: this can be done via the mass media or interpersonal communication.

7. *Choose the adequate form*: personal conversations, letters, posters, descriptive cards, brochures, photos, graphics, audio and video cassettes, etc.

8. *Carry out the planned action* while respecting the agenda.

9. *Evaluate the communication* beginning with three considerations: the work procedures, the impact that can be seen, and the perceived results.

---

[1] Address: Free Congress Foundation, 717 Second At., NE, Washington, D.C. 20002.

[2] *Comunicar las informaciones en materia de población y de planificación familiar a los responsables de tomar decisiones*. Series *Options for Population* (Washington: The Future Group International, 1994). One will find other indications of lobbying in *Gender Mapping. The European Union Trade Policy* (Brussels: WIDE, 1997) esp. 23-29; 42 f.

APPENDICES

APPENDIX I

AN UNEDITED LETTER
OF ALFRED SAUVY

FRENCH REPUBLIC
NATIONAL INSTITUTE FOR DEMOGRAPHIC STUDIES
27, RUE DU COMMANDER, 75675 PARIS - CEDEX 14
336.44.45 - TELEGRAPH ADDRESS: INEDEMO PARIS

Paris, Oct. 7, 1974

Monsieur M. Schooyans
My dear Colleague:

I thank you for your letter of Sept. 19 which I found upon my
return from Mexico. Abortion is consistent with the general line
of society's evolution; it is not out of tune and seems progres-
sive. In a general way, the Western populations are touched by
ageing in a fashion that does not affect their conscience. It is an
anesthetic and analgesic. All our decline results directly from
this ageing.

Confronted with this, the young people, I mean the young population, are much better armed; they can suffer in various ways,
even famine, but they will inevitably bear it, since they go on
with life.

Please accept, my dear colleague, my sincere best wishes.

Signed

Alfred Sauvy

APPENDIX II

A SELECTION OF WORKS ABOUT POPULATION CONTROL ORGANIZATIONS

Note: Organizations publishing materials which we mention here are generally disposed to send them to those who request them.

Beyond Promises. Governments in Motion. One Year after the Beijing Women's Conference (New York: WEDO, 1996; 355 Lexington Avenue). This comes from one of the most radical feminist movements.

Reed Boland, *Promoting Reproductive Rights: A Global Mandate* (New York: Center for Reproductive Law and Policy, 1997; 120 Wall St. 10005).

Shanti R. Conly, *Taking the Lead. The United Nations and Population Assistance* (Washington: Population Action International, 1996; 1120 19th St., Suite 550). Concerns the UN's leadership in population matters.

Conseil d'administration du programme de Nations Unies pour le développement et du Fonds de Nations Unies pour la population. Rapport du Conseil d'administration sur ses travaux en 1996 (New York: Economic and Social Council, 1996; E/1996/33, Supplement n. 13). This concerns above all UNPD and UNFPA.

Curenta años salvando vidas con planificación familiar. Informe de la Federación International de Planificación Familiar. Region de Hemisferio Occidental (New York: Planned Parenthood, 1994). This reports what this private organization has done, is doing and plans to do in Latin America, abundantly financed by public authorities. One will find more information at the headquarters of IPPF, Regent's College, Inner Circle, Regent's Park, London NW1 4NS, England.

117

Carl Djerassi, *The Politics of Contraception* (New York: Norton, 1979)- a reference that must not be overlooked.

Effective Family Programs (Washington: World Bank, 1993).

Estado de la Población Mundial, ed. Annually by Nafis Sadik (New York: UNFPA, 1998)

Excessive Force: Power, Politics and Population Control (Washington: Information Projects for Africa, P.O. 43345). It denounced especially the control of African populations.

Family Planning: A Development Success Story, 1994 (Washington: World Bank, 1994), a brochure summing up the activity of the World Bank.

Jason L. Finkle and C. Alison McIntosh (eds.), *The New Politics of Population, 1994* (New York: The Population Council, 1994). This is essential, for it explains the new "justifications" for family planning and correlated projects.

Cynthia Green, *Profiles of UN Organizations Working in Population* (Washington: Population Action International, 1996).

Polly Harrison and Allan Rosenfields (eds), *Contraceptive Research and Development. Looking to the Future* (Washington: National Academy Press, 1996)-a mine of information.

Betsy Hartmann, *Reproductive Rights and Wrongs. The Global Politics of Population Control*, 2nd ed. (Boston: South End Press, 1995)- as a rule, a critique of control programs.

Health and Environment in Sustainable Development. Five Years After the Earth Summit (Geneva: WHO, 1997).

High Stakes. The United States, Global Population and Our Common Future (New York: The Rockefeller Foundation, 1997)-the viewpoint of the North American establishment.

Inventory of Population Projects in Developing Countries Around the World, 1996, published about every two years by the UN's Population Fund (UNFPA). This is essential, for it contains a detailed chapter on what is done in every developing country to control population.

Stanley P. Johnson, *World Population and the United Nations. Challenge and Response* (Cambridge Univ. Press, 1987).

Monograph on Family Planning Associations' Activities (Dakar: St. Paul Press, 1989?)-detailed reports on each African country.

Population and Development. Directory of Nongovernmental Organizations in OEC Countries (Paris: OECD, 1994) -list of the organizations implicated in population policies.

Population and Development. Implications for the World Bank (Washington: The World Bank, 1994).

Population Growth and Economic Development: Policy Questions (Washington: National Academy Press, 1986)-reservations regarding the "necessity" of population control.

Rapport mondial sur le développement humain 1998 published by UNPD (Paris: Ed. Economica, 1998).

Rapport sur la santé dans le monde 1997 (Geneva: WHO, 1997).

Godfrey Roberts (ed.), *Population Policy. Contemporary Issues* (New York: Praeger, 1990)-explains diverse viewpoints.

Jorge Scala, "IPPF. La multinacional de la muerte," *Rosario* (Argentina)-one of the best critical studies of IPPF.

Statistiques de base 1996, published regularly by Eurostat (Brussels-Luxemburg, 1998).

Sustainable America. A New Consensus for Prosperity, Opportunity and Healthy Environment for the Future (Washington: The President's Council for Sustainable Development, 1996). It concerns the interests of the United States.

The Least Developed Countries 1997 Report (New York & Geneva: the UN Conference on Trade and Development, 1997).

The Life and Death of NSSM 200 [Kissinger Report] by Stephen Mumford. The text of the Report is found on pp. 47-186. This book is violently anti-Catholic and can be requested from the Center for Research on Population and Security, P.O. Box 13067, Research Triangle Park, NC 27709.

119

UNPD/UNFPA/WHO/World Bank, *HRP. Special Programme of Research-Development and Research Training in Human Reproduction.* Biennial Report 1994-1995 (Geneva: WHO, 1996)-basic.

Vision 2000 comprises many brochures in English, Spanish and French and was published by IPPF in London. Let us mention: *Plan Estratégico*, 1993; *Vision 2000 and the ICPD Programme of Action*, 1994; *IPPF Charter on Sexual and Reproductive Rights*, 1995; *Sexual and Reproductive Health. Family Planning Puts Promises into Practice*, 1995; etc.

Helen Wallace (ed.), *Health Care of Women and Children in Developing Countries*, 2nd ed. (Oakland, CA.: Third Party Publishing Co., 1995)-basic: contributions of the most famous population controllers.

World Abortion Policies 1994 (New York: Population Division of the UN, 1994)-data sheets.

World Bank Annual Report 1998 (Washington: World Bank, 1998).

World Contraceptive Use 1994 (New York: Population Division of the UN)-data sheets.

World Development Indicators 1997 (Washington: World Bank, 1997).

World Population Sheet 1999, published annually by the Population Reference Bureau, 1875 Connecticut Ave., NW, Suite 520, Washington DC 20009: internet site: <http://www.prb.org>.

World Population Monitoring 1996 (New York: Population Division of the UN, 1998).

World Population Plan of Action. 1994 Report (New York: UN, 1995).

World Population Prospects: The 1996 Revision. Annex I: *Demographic Indicators*; Annex II and III: *Demographic Indicators by Major Area, Region and Country* (New York; UN Population Division, 1996)-statistical data.

APPENDIX III

POPULATION ON INTERNET SITES

1. ORGANIZATIONS ENGAGING IN POPULATION CONTROL

a. *Public Organizations*:
— The USAID Development Information Services
http://www.info.usaid.gov

— UNPD/UNFPA/WHO/World Bank Special Program of
Research, Development and Research Training in Human
Reproduction
http://www.who.int/hrp/

— UNICEFF
http://www.unicef.org

— United Nations Development Program
http://www.undp.org

— United Nations Population Division
http://www.undp.org/popin/popin.htm

— United Nations Statistical Division
http://www.un.org/depts/unsd

— UN Population Fund
http://www.unfpa.org

— World Bank
http://www.worldbank.org

b. *Private Organizations*:
— Family Health International
http://www.fhi.org

— Ford Foundation
http://www.fordfound.org

— IPPF
http://www.oppf.org

— Johns Hopkins Population Center
http://www.jhsph.edu/Research/Centers/Population

— Johns Hopkins Program for International Education in Reproductive Health
http://www.jhpiego.jhu.edu

— JOICFP (Japanese Organization for International Cooperation in Family Planning))
http://www.bekkoame.or.jp/i/joicfp

— Marie Stopes International
http://www.mariestopes.org.uk

— Pathfinder International
http://www.pathfind.org

— Population Action International (PAI))
http://www.populationaction.org
See in particular the page devoted to links:
http://www.populationaction.org/special.links.htm

— The Alan Guttmacher Institute
http://www.agr-usa.org

— The John D. And Catherine T. MacArthur Foundation
http://www.macfdn.org

— The Population Council
http://www.popcouncil.org

— The World Watch Institute
http://www.worldwatch.org

— Women's Environmental & Development Organization
http://www.wedo.org

122

— Zero Population Growth, Inc.
  http://www.zpg.org

2. ORGANIZATIONS IN THE SERVICE OF THE "CULTURE OF LIFE"

— ACI-Digital
  http://www.aciprensa.com

— Africa 20000
  http://www.africa2000.com

— American Pro-life Network
  http://www.plnweb.com/indes.html (Has numerous links)

— Catholic Family and Human Rights Institute (CAFHRI))
  http:///www.cafhri.org

— Catholic Information Center on Internet
  http://www.catholic.net/rcc/loveboth/abortion_index.html

— Catholic Medical Association
  http://www.cathmed.com

— Escuela virtual para padres
  http://www.nalejandria.com

— Human Life International
  http://www.hli.org
  (In English, French, Spanish & Polish)

— Human Life International
  http://www.hli.org/french/index.html

— Le Feu
  http://perso.infonie.be/le.feu

— Life Institute (International Pro-Life Info)
  http://www.lifeinstitute.org

123

— Life-Site Daily News
  http://www.lifesite.net

— National Right to Life
  http://www/nrlc.org

— National Women's Coalition for Life
  http://sehlat.com/lifelink/ffl/plgroups.html

— Noticias de la ONUU
  http://www.pagina.de/noticiasdelaonu

— Pharmacists for Life International
  http://www.pfli.org

— Population Research Institute
  http://www.pop.org

— Pro-Life Infonet
  http://www.prolifeinfo.org.wcf

— Sisters of Life
  http://www.sistersoflife.org

— The RU-486 Files
  http://www.ru486.org

— The Ultimate Pro-Life List
  http://www.prolife.orgultimate
  (numerous links for English)

— Trans Vie-Net
  http://www.transvie.com

— Vinculum
  http://www.vinculum-news.com

— Zenit
  http://www.zenit.org

124

THE CALENDAR FOR 2000

Here are some of the events planned by the UN for the year 2000 in which there will be discussion of population, development, women, the rights of man. An asterisk indicates annual celebrations.

CONFERENCES AND CELEBRATIONS

In 2000: Celebration of the International Year for Peace

FEBRUARY

7-8   February, New York: Meeting of the Commission for Social Development.

MARCH

6-24   March, New York: Meeting of the Commission for the Status of Women, preparatory for the special session of the General Assembly (New York, June 5).

8   March: The UN Day for the Rights of Women and International Peace.*

21   March: International Day for the elimination of racial discrimination, followed by a week for Solidarity on the same theme.*

APRIL

3-14   April, New York: Meeting of the committee to prepare the special session of the General Assembly (Geneva, June 26-30).

7   April: World Day of Health.*

MAY

In May at Nairobi: Preparatory session for the special session of the General Assembly in June 2001, to verify the application of the resolutions of the Conference Habitat II (Istanbul, 1996).

15   May: World Family Day.*

Beginning with May 25: Week of solidarity with people of all the colonial territories fighting for freedom, independence and the rights of man.

JUNE

5   June: World Environment Day.*

5-9   June, New York: Special session of the General Assembly to verify the application of the Action Programs for Women determined during the World Conferences at Nairobi (1985) and Beijing (1995). Theme: "Women 2000: Gender Equality, Development and Peace."

26-30 June, Geneva: Special session of the General Assembly on the application of the decision reached at the World Summit for Social Development (Copenhagen 1995).

JULY

3-28   July, New York: Meeting of the Economic Social Council (ECOSOC).

11   July: World Population Day.*

AUGUST

9   August: International Day for the Indigenous Peoples of the World.*

SEPTEMBER

September, New York: Opening Day for the General Assembly; International Peace Day.*

September, New York: Millenium. Assembly of Peoples and Forum of the Nongovernmental Organizations.

16   September: International Day for the Preservation of the Ozone
      Layer.*

OCTOBER

1   October: International Day for the Aged.*

2   October: World Habitat Day.*

16   October: World Food Day.*

17   October: International Day for the Eradication of Poverty.

24   October: United Nations Day.*

NOVEMBER

16   November: International Tolerance Day.*

20   November: (variable date) Universal Children's Day.*

DECEMBER

1   December: World AIDS Day.*

3   December: World Handicapped Day.*

5   December: International Day for Voluntary Service toward
      Economic and Social Development.*

10   December: Rights of Man Day.*

DECENNIAL OBSERVANCES IN PREPARATION

1991-2000: 4th Decade of the UN on Development.

1993-2003: 3rd Decade against Racism and Discrimination.

1994-2004: International Decade for Indigenous Peoples.

1995-2004: UN's Decennial on Education for the Rights of Man.

1997-2006: UN's Decennial for the Eradication of Poverty.

Sources: http://www.un.org and News and Views (New York) vol. 11,
      n. 2 (June 1998) 19, which is a publication of the nongovern-
      mental feminist organization WEDO.

BIBLIOGRAPHY

"Ageing: The Surest Demographic Reality of the Next Century," *World Health* (Geneva) 2, 1998, 26 f.

Agency Performance Report 1996 (Washington: US Agency for International Development, January 1997).

America's Commitment: Federal Programs Benefiting Women and New Initiatives as Follow-up to the UN Fourth World Conference on Women (Washington: President's Council on Women, 1997).

Annual Report 1997 and 1998 (New York: Population Council).

Annual Technical Report 1997 and 1998, edited by P. F. A. Van Look (Geneva: WHO, 1998 and 1999).

Annual World Bank Conference on Development in Latin America and the Caribbean, 1996: Poverty and Inequality, Proceedings of a Conference Held at Bogotà, Columbia, edited by Shahid Javel Burki, SriRam Aiyer, Rudolf Hommes (Washington: World Bank, 1998).

Francis Baileux, "L'Etat de mariage toujours pénalisé: *La Libre Belgique* (Brussels) March 28, 1998, 25.

Gary Becker, *Human Capital* (New York: Columbia Univ. Press, 1964);—-*A Treatise on the Family* (Cambridge, MA: Harvard Univ. Press, 1993; 1st edit. 1981).

Jacques Bichot and Michael Godet, "Le tabou démographique," *Le Monde* (Paris) April 14, 1998.

Jean Bourgeois-Pichat, "Du XIXe siècle: l'Europe et sa population après l'an 2000," *Population* (Paris) 43, Jan-Feb 1989, 9-42.

Sulvie Brunel and Yves Blayo, "La mort des petites filles chinoises," *Le Monde* March 7, 1998.

Zbigniew Brzezinski, Between Two Ages: *America's Role in the Technetronic Era* (Harmondsworth: Penguin Books, 1970).

Jean-Claude Chesnais, *Le crépuscule de l'Occident. Denatalité, conditions des femmes et migrations* (Paris: Laffont, 1995).

Sophie Coignard and Anne Jeanblanc, "Organisation mondiale de la santé. Scandale et gabegies," *Le Point* (Paris) n. 1334, April 11, 1998, 82-89.

Comunicar la informaciones en materia de población y de planificación familiar a los responsables de tomar decisiones. Series: *Options for Population* (Washington: The Future Group International, 1994).

Michael Cook, *The New Imperialism. World Population and the Cairo Conference* (Crows Nest, NSW, Australia: Little Hills Press, 1994).

Deadly Exports. The Story of European Community Exports of Banned or Withdrawn Drugs to the Third World (Amsterdam: ED. WEMOS/Pharma Projects, 1991).

Maria Luisa Di Pietro and Roberta Minacori, "Sull'abortività della pillola estroprogestinica e di altri 'contracettivi'," *Medicina e Morale* (Rome) n. 5, 1996, 863-900.

Dossier d'Information sur la Population et le Développement (London: Marie Stopes International, 1994).

Richard Dubreuil, "Denatalité: le piège se referme," *L'Homme Nouveau* (Paris) 1189-1190, Aug 2-16, 1998, 1 and 3.

Gerard-François Dumont, "Démographie et analyse stratégique," *Défense*, 83 (March 1999) 76-80.

—*Les spécificités démographiques des régions et l'aménagment du territoires* (Paris: Ed. Des Journaux officiels, 1996).

—*Le monde et les hommes. Les grandes évolutions démographiques* (Paris: Ed. Litec, 1995)

—*Démographie* (Paris: Ed. Dunod, 1992).

—*Le Festin du Kronos* (Paris: Ed. Fleurus, 1991).—*Pour la liberté familiale* (Paris: PUF, 1986).

—*La France ridée. Echapper à la logique du déclin* (Paris: Ed. Le Livre de poche, 8335E, 1979).

129

Jacques Dupâquier, "L'Europe malade de sa démographie," *Population et Avenir* (Paris) n. 643, May-June 1999, 2 f.

Gregg Esterbrook, "Forgotten Benefactor of Humanity," *The Atlantic Monthly* January 1997, 75-82.

Nicholas Eberstadt, "World Population Implosion?" *Human Life Review* 24, n. 1 (Winter, 1998) 15-30.

Rudolf Ehmann, "Problems in Family Planning," *Anthropotes* (Rome) n. 1 (1991) 95-126.

Paul and Anne Ehrlich, *Ecoscience, Population, Resources and Environment* (New York: W. H. Freeman, 1977).

"El consentimiento informada," *Cuadernos de Bioetica* (Santiago de Compostela) 9, 33, la, 1998.

Etat de la population mondiale 1998 (New York: UNFPA, 1998).

Imogen Evans and Carlos Huezo (eds.), *Family Planning Handbook for Health Professionals. The Sexual and Reproductive Approach* (London, IPPF, 1997).

Expert Group Meeting on Below-Replacement Fertility by Population Division, Department of Economic and Social Affairs (New York: UN, November 4-6, 1997) UN/POP/BRF/BP/1997/1.

Manuel Ferrer Regales and Juan José Calvo Miranda, *Declive demográfico, Cambio urbano y Crisis rural. Las trasformaciones recientes de la población de España* (Pamplona: Ed. Universidad de Navarra [EUNSA], 1994).

Luc Ferry, *Le nouvel ordre écologique* (Paris: Le Livre de Poche, 13565, 1998).

John Kenneth Galbraith, *La République des satisfaits. La culture du contentement aux Etats Unis* (Paris: Seuil, 1993).

Carlo Gallucci, "La Pillola Maldetta," *L'Espresso* (Rome) Oct. 20, 1991, 156-165.

François Geinoz (ed.), *Europe. L'hiver démographique* (Lausanne: Ed. Age d'homme, 1989).

130

BIBLIOGRAPHY

Alene Gelbard, Carl Haub, Mary M. Kent, *World Population Beyond
   Six Billion*, installment of the Population Bulletin, 54, 1, March
   1999 (Washington: Population Reference Bureau, 1999).

Gender Mapping. The European Union Trade Policy (Brussels:
   Women in Development Europe, 1997).

Grantmaking Guidelines, Pre-publication draft (Chicago: MacArthur
   Foundation, 1997?).

Cynthia Green (ed.), *Profiles of UN Organizations* (Washington:
   Population Action International, 1996).

Seamus Grimes, "From Population Control to 'Reproductive Rights':
   Ideological Influences in Population Policy," *Third World
   Quarterly* 19, 3 (1998) 375-393.

Guide des responsables des programmes de planification familiale,
   prepared by Management Sciences for Health and Pathfinder
   International (West Hartford, CT: Kumarian Press, 1994).

Polly Harrison and Allan Rosenfield (eds.), *Contraceptive Research
   and Development. Looking to the Future* (Washington: National
   Academy Press, 1996).

Betsy Hartmann, *Reproductive Rights and Wrongs. The Global
   Politics of Population Control*, 2nd ed. (Boston: South End
   Press, 1995).

*Health and Environment in Sustainable Development. Five Years after
   the Earth Summit* (Geneva: WHO, 1997).

Health, Nutrition and Population (Washington: World Bank Group,
   The Human Development Network, 1997).

Stanley P. Johnson, *World Population and the United Nations*
   (Cambridge Univ. Press, 1987).

La population mondiale en mutation, Le Monde Dossiers et
   Documents (Paris) 227, June 1999.

Yves-Marie Laulan, *Les Nations suicidaires* (Paris: de Guibert, 1998).

Elizabeth Liagin, *Excessive Force: Power, Politics and Population
   Control* (Washington: Ed. Informations Project for Africa,
   1995).

Milos Macura, "The Significance of the United Nations International Population Conferences," *Population Bulletin of the UN* n. 19/20 (1986) 14-25.

Yves Mamou, "Le vieillissement, source de déclin?" *Le Monde Economique* (Paris) April 7, 1998, I-III.

Laure Mandeville, "La Russie sera le 'pays des veuves'," *Le Figaro* July 2,1999.

Charles Mann, "Reseeding the Green Revolution," *Science* 277 (Aug. 22, 1997 1038-1043.

George Martine, "Brazil's Fertility Decline," *Population and Development Review* (New York) 22, 1 (March 1996) 47-75.

Carl J. Marucci (ed.), *Serving the Human Family. The Holy See at the Major UN Conferences* (New York: The Path of Peace Foundation, 1997).

Peter McDonald, *Gender Equity, Social Institutions and the Future of Fertility* (Canberra: Australian National University, Working Papers on Demography, n. 69, 1997).

Etienne de Montety, "Voici la vérité: la natalité ne se redresse pas. Le cri d'alarme des démographes," *Le Figaro*, 799 (Feb. 17, 1996) 28-35.

Stephen D. Mumford, *The Life and Death of NSSM 200* (Center for Research on Population and Security, PO Box 13067, Research Triangle Park, NC 27709, 1994).

Daniel Noin, *Atlas de la population mondiale* (Montpellier: Ed. Reclus, 1991).

Peter G. Peterson "Gray Dawn: The Global Aging Crisis," *Foreign Affairs* 78, 1 (Jan.-Feb. 1999).

Jorge del Pinal and Andrey Singer, "Generation of Diversity: Latinos in the United States," *Population Bulletin* 52, 3 (Oct. 1997) 16 f.

Población, Salud reproductiva y probreza document of the comision Economica para America Latina y el Caribe (CEPAL), 27th session, Oranjestad, Aruba, May 11-16, 1998, side LC/G.2015 (SE 5.27/20), 98-2-188, April 15, 1998.

Politiques de coopération du développement à l'horizon 2000, collection published in Brussels and Luxemburg by the Commission of European Communities, 1996.

"Projet de déclaration sur les défenseurs de droits de l'homme," *Le Monde* December 8, 1998, 19.

Rapport annuel 1997-1998 (London: IPPF).

Rapports annuels 1997 et 1998 (Washington: World Bank).

Rapport mondial sur le développement humain. 1998, published by UNPD (Paris: Ed. Economica, 1998).

Reproductive Health. Directory of Training Courses (New York: UNFPA, 1996/1997).

Resource Requirements for Population and Reproductive Health Programs (New York: UNFPA, 1996).

Fenneke Reysoo, Anke van der Kwaak and Nasreen Huq, *The Incentive Trap. A Study on Coercion, Reproductive Rights and Women's Anatomy in Bangladesh* (Leiden: Rijks Universiteit, 1995).

Renauld de Rochebrune, "Population. En route vers les 10 milliards," *Jeune Afrique* (Paris) Oct. 27-Nov. 2, 1998, 46-53.

Rafael M. Salas, *Reflections on Population* (New York: Pergamon, 1986).

Arturo Salazar Larraín, "¿El exterminio de la poblacion rural?" *El Comercio* (Lima) Feb. 23, 1998.

—"Silencio irresponsable," *El Comercio*, April 2, 1998.

—"¿Quien responde por las campañas de esterilizacion y sus excesos?" *El Comercio*, April 3, 1998.

Juan Claudio Sanahuja, *El grand desafío. La Cultura de la Vida contra la Cultura de la Muerte* (Buenos Aires: Ed. Serviam, 1995).

Amartya Sen, *L'Economie est une science morale* (Paris: Ed. La Découverte, 1999).

George S. Simmons and Ghazi M. Farooq, *Fertility in Developing Countries. An Economic Perspective on Research and Policy Issues* (London: Macmillan, 1985).

Julian Simon, *L'homme, notre dernière chance* (Paris: PUF, 1985).

— *Population and Development in Poor Countries* (Princeton Univ. Press, 1991).

Simon Stanley and Sara Hyde, *Handbook on European Union Support for Population and Reproductive Health Programmes* (New York: UNFPA and London: Marie Stopes International, 1995).

Linda Stark, Lester R. Brown, et al., Vital Signs 1997. *The Environmental Trends That Are Shaping Our Future* (New York: The Worldwatch Institute and W. W. Norton Co., 1997).

The Least Developed Countries. 1997 Report UNCTAD (New York and Geneva: UN, 1997).

"The Population Implosion," *Wall Street Journal*, Oct. 16, 1997; distributed by e-mail: Family@upbeat.com

Alvin Toffler, *Les Nouveaux pouvoirs* (Paris: Fayard, 1991).

UNDP/UNFPA/WHO/World Bank, *Special programme of Research, Development and Research Training in Human Reproduction. Reproductive Health Research: The New Directions. Report 1996-1997,* 25th Anniversary issue, ed. by J. Khanna and P. F. A. Van Look (Geneva: WHO, 1998).

Rose Linda G. Valenzona, "Demographic Trends in Selected Countries in the Asia and Pacific Region," *International Conference on Demography and the Family in Asia and Oceania*, Acts of the Congress of Taipei, Sept. 18-20, 1995 (Taipei, 1996) 89-119.

—-*The Empty Cradles of Asia* (Manila: mimeographed, 1995?).

Ben J. Wattenberg, "*The Population Explosion is Over*," *New York Times Magazine*, Nov. 23, 1997.

World Population Monitoring. 1996. Selected Aspects of Reproductive Rights and Reproductive Health (New York: UN, 1998).

World Population Prospects: The 1996 Revision. Draft (New York: UN: three volumes: 1. The text itself, dated January 1998 and side ESA/P/WP.138; 2. Appendix I, *Demographic Indicators*, dated October 24, 1996; 3. Appendix II and III, *Demographic Indicators by Major Area, Region and Country*, dated October 1997.

INDEX OF NAMES

SUBJECT INDEX

139